Berlitz®

The world at your fingertips

French

picture dictionary

www.berlitzpublishing.com

Distribution
UK, Ireland and Europe:
Apa Publications (UK) Ltd;
sales@insightguides.com
United States and Canada:
Ingram Publisher Services;
ips@ingramcontent.com
Australia and New Zealand:
Woodslane; info@woodslane.com.au
Southeast Asia:
Apa Publications (SN) Pte;
singaporeoffice@insightguides.com
Hong Kong, Taiwan and China:
Apa Publications (HK) Ltd;
hongkongoffice@insightguides.com
Worldwide: Apa Publications (UK) Ltd;
sales@insightguides.com

Special Sales, Content Licensing and CoPublishing
Insight Guides can be purchased in bulk quantities at discounted prices. We can create special editions, personalised jackets and corporate imprints tailored to your needs. sales@insightguides.com; www.insightguides.biz

First Edition 2017

Printed in China by CTPS

Contact us
Every effort has been made to provide accurate information in this publication, but changes are inevitable. The publisher cannot be responsible for any resulting loss, inconvenience or injury. We would appreciate it if readers would call our attention to any errors or outdated information. We also welcome your suggestions; please contact us at: berlitz@apaguide.co.uk

Series Editor: Carine Tracanelli
Editor: Urszula Krajewska
Head of Production: Rebeka Davies
Series design: Krzysztof Kop
Picture research & DTP design: Tamkapress
English text: Carine Tracanelli & Barbara Marchwica
Translation: Carine Tracanelli
Simplified phonetics: ILS AT
Photo credits: all Shutterstock and Fotolia

Introduction

Whether you are a total beginner or already have a sound knowledge of your chosen language, this Berlitz picture dictionary will help you to communicate quickly and easily. Packed with 2,000 useful terms, it covers all everyday situations, whether you're applying for a job, going shopping or just getting around. See, understand, memorise: visual learning by combining a word with an image helps you remember it more effectively as images affect us more than text alone.

To get the most out of your picture dictionary you can search for words in two ways: by theme (women's clothes, sporting facilities, hobbies, etc.) or by consulting the index at the end. You'll also find important phrases surrounding a topic in each chapter, ensuring that you have the foundations you need for communicating.

Each word is followed by its phonetic transcription to make sure you pronounce each word or sentence correctly. You will find a helpful guide to pronunciation in your chosen language on pages 7–9.

Note that the terms in this picture dictionary are always given in their singular form unless they are generally only used in their plural form, and all nouns are preceded by their gender-specific article. Certain terms are not gender-neutral and in such cases all genders are provided throughout in both the translation and phonetic transcription, ensuring you can communicate in all variants.

Berlitz are renowned for the quality and expertise of their language products. Discover the full range at www.berlitzpublishing.com.

Table of Contents

Pronunciation

This section is designed to make you familiar with the sounds of French using our simplified phonetic transcription. You'll find the pronunciation of the French letters and sounds explained below, together with their "imitated" equivalents. This system is used throughout this dictionary; simply read the pronunciation as if it were English, noting any special rules below.

The French language contains nasal vowels, which are indicated in the pronunciation by a vowel symbol followed by an N. This N should not be pronounced strongly, but it is there to show the nasal quality of the previous vowel. A nasal vowel is pronounced simultaneously through the mouth and the nose.

In French, the final consonants of words are not always pronounced. When a word ending in a consonant is followed with a word beginning with a vowel, the two words are often run together. The consonant is therefore pronounced as if it begins the following word.

In our dictionary words are divided into syllables separated by hyphens and the last syllable, which is always stressed in French, is written in capital letters. The article is usually pronounced as if it is an integral part of the noun it precedes, and for that reason we note it in the pronunciation column as if it is the first syllable of the word.

Example	Pronunciation
comment	koh-MAWN
Comment allez-vous ?	koh-MAWN tah-lay-VOO ?

Letter	Approximate pronunciation	Symbol	Example	Pronunciation
cc	1. before e, i, like cc in accident	ks	**accessible**	ahk-seh-see-BLUH
	2. elsewhere, like cc in accommodate	k	**d'accord**	dah-KOHR
ch	like sh in shut	sh	**chercher**	shehr-SHAY
ç	like s in sit	s	**ça**	sah

Letter	Approximate pronunciation	Symbol	Example	Pronunciation
g	1. before e, i, y, like s in pleisure	zh	**manger**	mawn-ZHAY
	2. before a, o, u, like g in go	g	**garçon**	gahr-SOH
h	always silent		**homme**	ohm
j	like s in pleisure	zh	**jamais**	zhah-MAY
qu	like k in kill	k	**qui**	kee
r	rolled in the back of the mouth, like gargling	r	**rouge**	roozh
w	usually like v in voice	v	**wagon**	vah-GOH

b, c, d, f, k, l, m, n, p, s, t, v, x and z are pronounced as in English.

Vowels

Letter	Approximate pronunciation	Symbol	Example	Pronunciation
a, à, â	between the a in hat and the a in father	ah	**mari**	mah-REE
e	sometimes like a in about	uh	**je**	zhuh
è, ê, e	like e in get	eh	**même**	mehm

é, ez	like a in late	ay	**été**	ay-TAY
i	like ee in meet	ee	**il**	eel
o, ô	generally like o in roll	oh	**donner**	doh-NAY
u	like ew in dew	ew	**une**	ewn

Sounds spelled with two or more letters

Letter	Approximate pronunciation	Symbol	Example	Pronunciation
ai, ay, aient, ais, ait, aî, ei	like a in late	ay	**j'ai**	zhay
			vais	vay
ai, ay,	like e in get	eh	**chaîne**	shehn
aient, ais, ait, aî, ei			**peine**	pehn
(e)au	similar to o	oh	**chaud**	shoh
eu, eû,	like u in fur but short	uh	**euro**	uh-ROH
œu	like a puff of air			
euil, euille	like uh + y	uhy	**feuille**	fuhy
ail, aille	like ie in tie	ie	**taille**	tie
ille	1. like yu in yucca	eeyuh	**famille**	fah-MEEYUH
	2. like eel	eel	**ville**	veel
oi, oy	like w followed by the a in hat	wah	**moi**	mwah
ou, oû	like o in move or o in hoot	oo	**nouveau**	noo-VOH
ui	approximately like wee in between	wee	**traduire**	trah-DWEER

GENERAL VOCABULARY

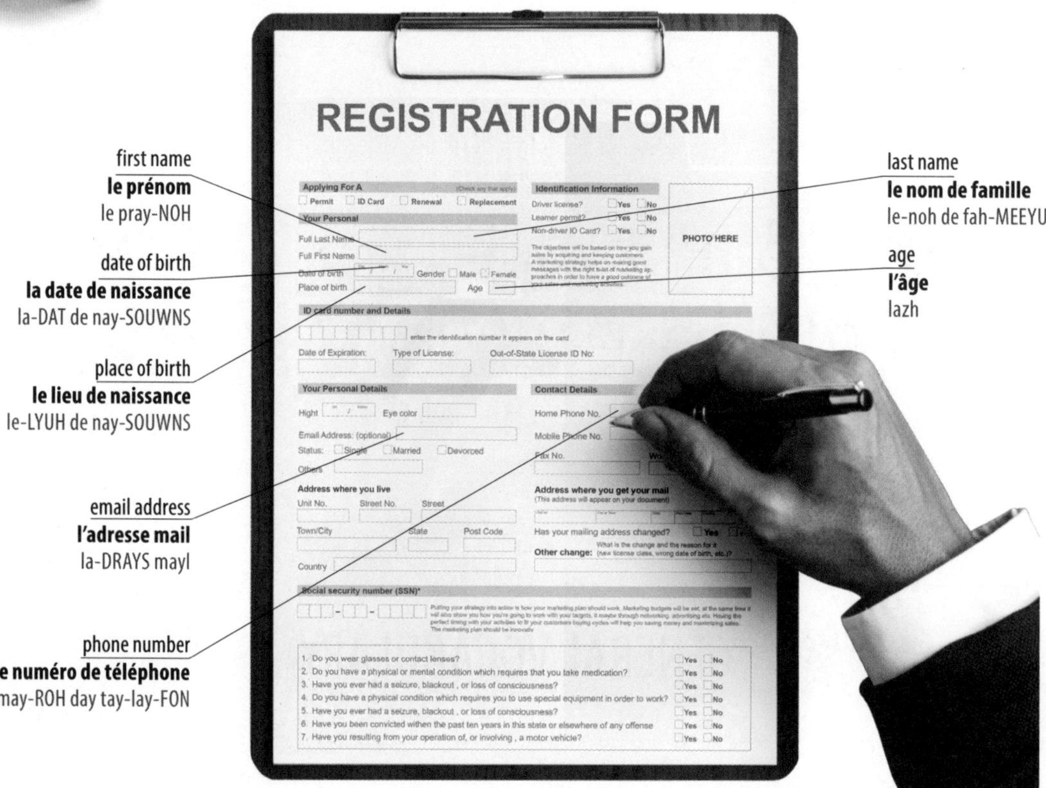

first name
le prénom
le pray-NOH

date of birth
la date de naissance
la-DAT de nay-SOUWNS

place of birth
le lieu de naissance
le-LYUH de nay-SOUWNS

email address
l'adresse mail
la-DRAYS mayl

phone number
le numéro de téléphone
le nu-may-ROH day tay-lay-FON

last name
le nom de famille
le-noh de fah-MEEYUH

age
l'âge
lazh

address	**l'adresse**	la-DRAYS
marital status	**l'état civil**	lay-TAH see-VEEL
children	**les enfants**	le-zawn-FOUWN
home country	**le pays d'origine**	le pay-EEH doh-ree-ZHEEN
place of residence	**le lieu de résidence**	le-LYUH de ray-zee-DAHNS
single	**célibataire**	say-lee-ba-TAYR
in a relationship	**en couple**	uh-KOOPL
divorced	**divorcé *m* / divorcée *f***	dee-vor-SAY / dee-vor-SAY
married	**marié *m* / mariée *f***	ma-ree-YAI / Ma-ree-YAI
widowed	**veuf *m* / veuve *f***	VUHF / VUHV
What's your name?	**Comment vous appelez-vous ?**	koh-MAWN voo-za-PLAY-VOO ?
Where are you from?	**D'où êtes-vous ?**	doo eht-VOO ?
Where were you born?	**Où êtes-vous né *m* / née *f* ?**	oo eht-VOO nay ?
When were you born?	**Quand êtes-vous né *m* / née *f* ?**	kouw et-VOO nih ?
What is your address?	**Quelle est votre adresse ?**	kay-LAY votr ah-DRAIS ?
What's your phone number?	**Quel est votre numéro de téléphone ?**	kay-LAY votr new-may-ROH day tay-lay-FON ?
Are you married?	**Êtes-vous marié *m* / mariée *f* ?**	eht-VOO ma-ree-YAY / ma-ree-YAY ?
Do you have children	**Avez-vous des enfants ?**	a-vay-VOO day-zawn-FOUW ?

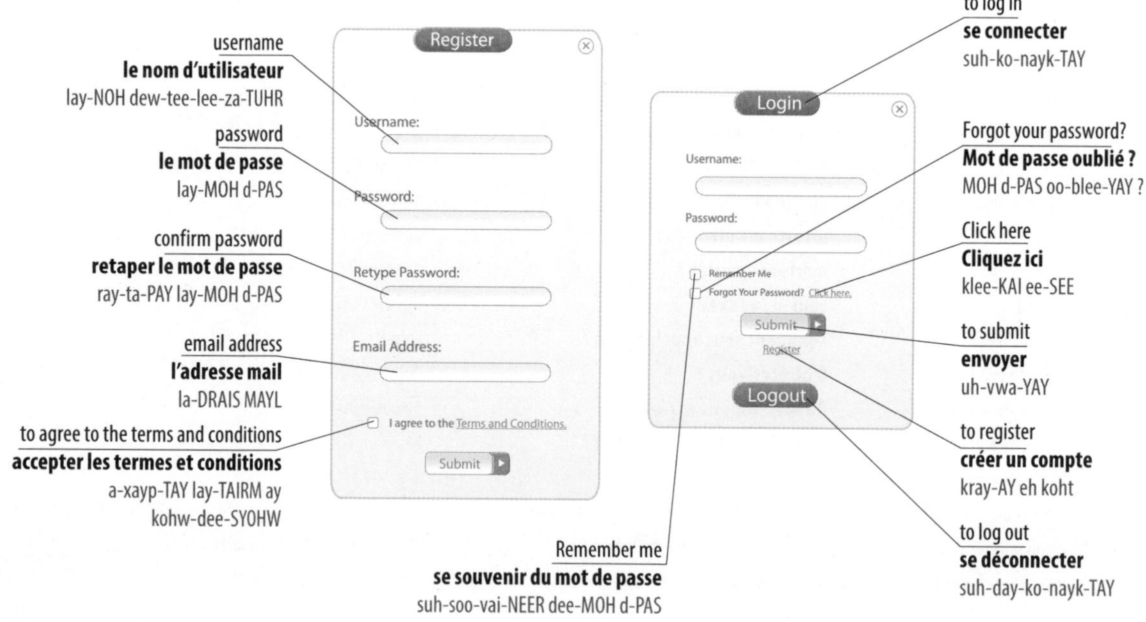
username
le nom d'utilisateur
lay-NOH dew-tee-lee-za-TUHR
password
le mot de passe
lay-MOH d-PAS
confirm password
retaper le mot de passe
ray-ta-PAY lay-MOH d-PAS
email address
l'adresse mail
la-DRAIS MAYL
to agree to the terms and conditions
accepter les termes et conditions
a-xayp-TAY lay-TAIRM ay kohw-dee-SYOHW
Register
Username:
Password:
Retype Password:
Email Address:
I agree to the Terms and Conditions.
Submit
Login
Username:
Password:
Remember Me
Forgot Your Password? Click here.
Submit
Register
Logout
to log in
se connecter
suh-ko-nayk-TAY
Forgot your password?
Mot de passe oublié ?
MOH d-PAS oo-blee-YAY ?
Click here
Cliquez ici
klee-KAI ee-SEE
to submit
envoyer
uh-vwa-YAY
to register
créer un compte
kray-AY eh koht
to log out
se déconnecter
suh-day-ko-nayk-TAY
Remember me
se souvenir du mot de passe
suh-soo-vai-NEER dee-MOH d-PAS

0 1 2 3 4 5 6 7 8 9

0	zero	**zéro**	zay-ROH
1	one	**un**	eh
2	two	**deux**	duh
3	three	**trois**	trwa
4	four	**quatre**	katr
5	five	**cinq**	sehk
6	six	**six**	seez
7	seven	**sept**	sayt
8	eight	**huit**	weet
9	nine	**neuf**	nuhf
10	ten	**dix**	deez
11	eleven	**onze**	ohz
12	twelve	**douze**	dooz
13	thirteen	**treize**	trayz
14	fourteen	**quatorze**	ka-TORZ
15	fifteen	**quinze**	kehz
16	sixteen	**seize**	sez

17	seventeen	**dix-sept**	deez-SAYT
18	eighteen	**dix-huit**	deez-WEET
19	nineteen	**dix-neuf**	deez-NUHF
20	twenty	**vingt**	veh
21	twenty-one	**vingt et un**	veh-tay-EH
30	thirty	**trente**	trawnt
40	forty	**quarante**	ka-ROUNT
50	fifty	**cinquante**	seh-KOUNT
60	sixty	**soixante**	swa-SOUNT
70	seventy	**soixante-dix**	swa-sount-DEEZ
80	eighty	**quatre-vingts**	katr-VEH
90	ninety	**quatre-vingt-dix**	katr-veh-DEEZ
100	one hundred	**cent**	suh
101	one hundred and one	**cent un**	suh-EH
1000	one thousand	**mille**	meey
1 000 000	one million	**un million**	eh mee-lee-OH

1st (first)
premier *m*/ première *f*
pruh-myay / pruh-myayr

2nd (second)
deuxième / second *m* seconde *f*
deh-zyaym / suh-koh / suh-kohd

3rd (third)
troisième
trwa-zyaym

4th	fourth	**quatrième**	ka-tryaym
5th	fifth	**cinquième**	seh-kyaym
6th	sixth	**sixième**	see-zyaym
7th	seventh	**septième**	say-tyaym
8th	eighth	**huitième**	wee-tyaym
9th	ninth	**neuvième**	nuh-vyaym
10th	tenth	**dixième**	dee-zyaym
11th	eleventh	**onzième**	oh-zyaym
12th	twelfth	**douzième**	doo-zyaym
13th	thirteenth	**treizième**	tray-zyaym
14th	fourteenth	**quatorzième**	ka-tor-zyaym
15th	fifteenth	**quinzième**	keh-zyaym
16th	sixteenth	**seizième**	say-zyaym
17th	seventeenth	**dix-septième**	deez-say-tyaym
18th	eighteenth	**dix-huitième**	deez-wee-tyaym
19th	nineteenth	**dix-neuvième**	deez-neh-vyaym
20th	twentieth	**vingtième**	veh-tyaym

21st	twenty-first	**vingt et unième**	veh-tay-ew-nyaym
22nd	twenty-second	**vingt-deuxième**	veh-deh-zyaym
23rd	twenty-third	**vingt-troisième**	veh-trza-zyaym
24th	twenty-fourth	**vingt-quatrième**	veh-ka-tryaym
25th	twenty-fifth	**vingt-cinquième**	veh-seh-kyaym
26th	twenty-sixth	**vingt-sixième**	veh-see-zyaym
27th	twenty-seventh	**vingt-septième**	veh-suh-tyaym
28th	twenty-eighth	**vingt-huitième**	veh-zee-tyaym
29th	twenty-ninth	**vingt-neuvième**	veh-neh-vyaym
30th	thirtieth	**trentième**	trawn-tyaym
40th	fortieth	**quarantième**	ka-rawn-tyaym
50th	fiftieth	**cinquantième**	seh-kouw-tyaym
60th	sixtieth	**soixantième**	swa-souw-tyaym
70th	seventieth	**soixante-dixième**	swa-souwt-dee-zyaym
80th	eightieth	**quatre-vingtième**	katr-veh-tyaym
90th	ninetieth	**quatre-vingt-dixième**	katr-veh-dee-zyaym
100th	hundredth	**centième**	sawn-tyaym

noon	**midi**	mee-DEE
midnight	**minuit**	mee-NWEE

one am	**une heure**	ew-NEHR
one pm	**treize heures**	tray-ZEHR

two am	**deux heures**	deh-ZEHR
two pm	**quatorze heures**	ka-TOR-ZEHR

three am	**trois heures**	trwa-ZEHR
three pm	**quinze heures**	keh-ZEHR

four am	**quatre heures**	ka-TREHR
four pm	**seize heures**	say-ZEHR

five am	**cinq heures**	seh-KEHR
five pm	**dix-sept heures**	deez-SAYT-EHR

six am	**six heures**	see-ZEHR
six pm	**dix-huit heures**	deez-WEE-TEHR

seven am	**sept heures**	say-TEHR
seven pm	**dix-neuf heures**	deez-NUH-VEHR

eight am	**huit heures**	wee-TEHR
eight pm	**vingt heures**	veh-TEHR

nine am	**neuf heures**	neh-VEHR
nine pm	**vingt-et-une heures**	veh-tay-EW-NEHR

ten am	**dix heures**	dee-ZEHR
ten pm	**vingt-deux heures**	veht-DUH-ZEHR

eleven am	**onze heures**	oh-ZEHR
eleven pm	**vingt-trois heures**	veht-TRWA-ZEHR

quarter to
moins le quart
mweh luh-KAR

ten to
moins dix
mweh deez

five to
moins cinq
mweh sehk

. . . o'clock
. . . heure(s)
. . . EHR

five past
. . . heures cinq
. . . ehr sehk

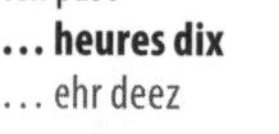

ten past
. . . heures dix
. . . ehr deez

quarter past
et quart
ay-KAR

half past
et demie
ay duh-MEE

What time is it?	**Quelle heure est-il ?**	kay-LEHR ay-teel ?
It's nine thirty.	**Il est neuf heures et demie.**	ee-lay neh-VEHR ay duh-MEE
Excuse me, could you tell me the time please?	**Excusez-moi, pourriez-vous me dire l'heure s'il vous plaît ?**	ayx-kew-zay-MWA, poo-ryay-voo muh deer lehr seel-voo-PLAY ?
It's about half past nine.	**Il est environ neuf heures et demie.**	ee-lay awn-vee-roh neh-VEHR ay-duh-MEE

Monday
lundi
leh-DEE

Tuesday
mardi
mar-DEE

Wednesday
mercredi
mayr-kray-DEE

Thursday
jeudi
zheh-DEE

Friday
vendredi
vawn-dray-DEE

Saturday
samedi
sam-DEE

Sunday
dimanche
dee-MAUWSH

on Monday	**lundi**	leh-DEE
from Tuesday	**à partir de mardi**	a-par-TEER deh mar-DEE
until Wednesday	**jusqu'à mercredi**	zhews-KOH mayr-kray-DEE

JANUARY
January
janvier
zhawn-VYAY

FEBRUARY
February
février
fay-VRYAY

MARCH
March
mars
mars

APRIL
April
avril
a-VREEL

MAY
May
mai
may

JUNE
June
juin
zheh

JULY
July
juillet
zhwee-YAY

AUGUST
August
août
oot

SEPTEMBER
September
septembre
sayp-TEHBR

OCTOBER
October
octobre
ok-TOBR

NOVEMBER
November
novembre
no-VEHBR

DECEMBER
December
décembre
day-SEHBR

in July	**en juillet**	awn zhwee-YAY
since September	**depuis septembre**	duh-PWEE sayp-TEHBR
until October	**jusqu'en octobre**	zhews-kaw-no-KTOBR
for two months	**pour deux mois**	poor duh mwa

morning	late morning	noon	afternoon	evening	night
le matin	**la fin de matinée**	**le midi**	**l'après-midi**	**le soir**	**la nuit**
luh ma-TEH	la-feh duh-ma-tee-NAY	luh-mee-DEE	la-pray-mee-DEE	luh-SWAR	la-NWEE

in the morning	**en matinée**	awn ma-tee-NAY
in the evening	**dans la soirée**	douw la-swa-RAY
in the night	**dans la nuit**	douw la-NWEE

cash
l'argent liquide
lar-ZHAWN lee-KEED

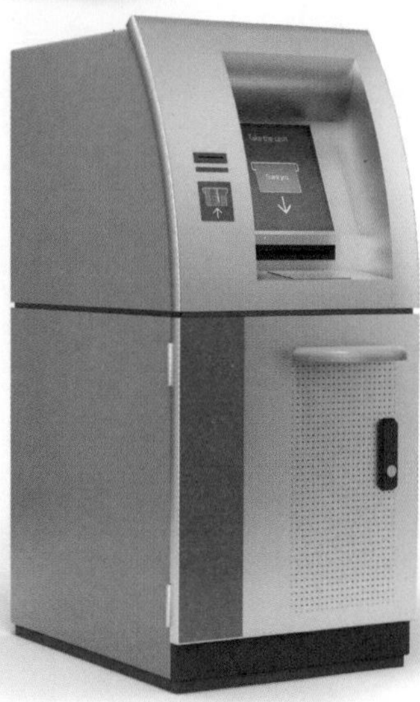

ATM / cashpoint
le distributeur automatique de billets
luh-dee-stree-bew-TEHR oh-toh-ma-TEEK duh-bee-YAY

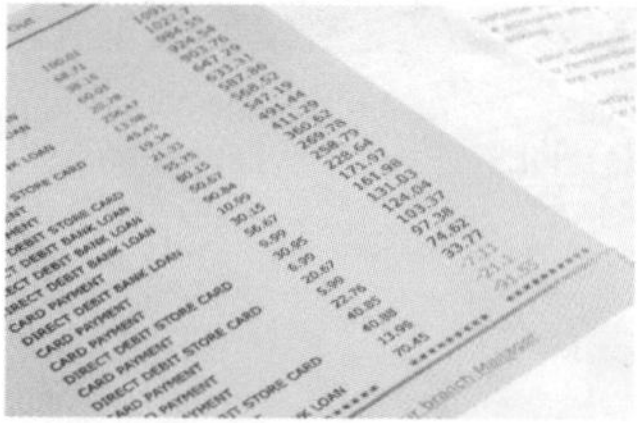

bank statement
le relevé bancaire
luh-reh-lay-VAY bouw-KAYR

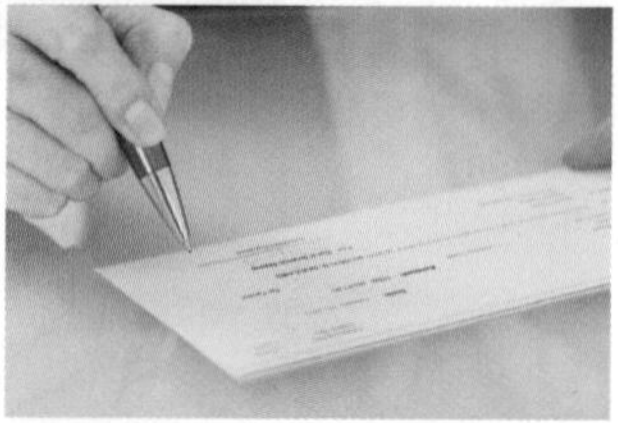

cheque
le chèque
luh-SHAYK

account	**le compte**	luh-KOHT
bank	**la banque**	la-BOUWK
bank charges	**les frais bancaires**	lay-FRAY bouw-KAYR
debit card	**la carte bancaire**	la-KART bouw-KAYR
debt	**la dette**	la-DAYT
current account	**le compte courant**	luh-koht koo-ROUW
loan	**le prêt**	luh-PRAY
mortgage	**le prêt immobilier**	luh-PRAY ee-mo-bee-LYAY
savings account	**le compte d'épargne**	luh-koht day-PARNY
standing order	**le prélèvement automatique**	luh-pay-lay-veh-MAWN o-toh-ma-TEEK

credit card
la carte de crédit
la-KART duh-kray-DEE

to borrow money	**emprunter de l'argent**	eh-preh-TAY deh lar-ZHAWN
to invest	**investir**	eh-vays-TEER
to lend money	**prêter de l'argent**	pray-TAY deh lar-ZHAWN
to pay	**payer**	pay-YAY
to take out a loan	**contracter un emprunt**	kon-trak-TAY eh awn-PREH
to withdraw from the account	**retirer du compte**	ray-tee-RAY dew-KOHT
to take out a mortgage	**contracter un prêt immobilier**	kon-trak-TAY eh-PRAY ee-mo-bee-LYAY
to withdraw	**retirer**	ray-tee-RAY

to save
épargner
ay-par-NYAY

Pound Sterling
la livre sterling
la-LEEVR stay-RLEENG

Euro
l'euro
luh-ROH

Dollar
le dollar
luh-doh-LAR

Franc
le franc
luh-FROUW

Yen
le yen
luh-JAYN

Won
le won
luh-WON

Yuan
le yuan
luh-yoo-OUN

Indian Rupee
la roupie indienne
la-roo-PEE eh-DYAYN

Zloty
le zloty
luh-zlo-TAY

Ruble
le rouble
luh-ROOBL

Leu
le leu
luh-LEH

Forint
le forint
luh-foh-REH

Shilling	**le shilling**	luh-shee-LEENG
Dirham	**le dirham**	luh-deer-HAM
Rial	**le rial**	luh-RYAL
Dong	**le dong**	luh-DONG
Krone	**la couronne**	la-koo-RON
Peso	**le peso**	luh-peh-SOH
Pound	**la livre**	la-LEEVR
Dinar	**le dinar**	luh-dee-NAR

exchange rate	**le taux de change**	luh-TOH duh-SHOUNZH
exchange rate for US Dollars to Japanese Yen	**le taux de change du dollar américain par rapport au yen japonais**	luh-TOH duh-SHOUNZH dew doh-LAR a-may-ree-KAH pa-ra-POR oh yayn zha-poh-NAY
foreign exchange	**l'échange de devises**	lay-SHOUNZH duh-duh-VEEZ
foreign exchange rate	**le cours des devises**	luh-KOOR day-duh-VEEZ

PEOPLE

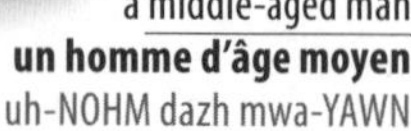

a middle-aged man
un homme d'âge moyen
uh-NOHM dazh mwa-YAWN

an old man
un vieil homme
uh vyeh-YOHM

a young woman
une jeune femme
ewn-ZHEHN fam

a young man
un jeune homme
uh-zheh-NOHM

baby
le bébé
luh-bay-BAY

a teenage girl
une adolescente
ewn-a-doh-les-SAWNT

a teenage boy
un adolescent
eh-na-doh-leh-SAWN

a young boy
un jeune garçon
uh-ZHEHN gar-SOH

child	**un enfant**	eh-nawn-FOUW
teenager	**l'adolescent**	la-doh-leh-SAWN
a young girl	**une jeune fille**	ewn-ZHEHN feey
a seven-year-old girl	**une fille de sept ans**	ewn-FEEY deh set-OUW
young	**jeune**	zhehn
a little boy	**un petit garçon**	eh peh-TEE gar-SOH
a little girl	**une petite fille**	ewn peh-TEET feey
middle-aged	**d'âge moyen**	dazh mwa-YAWN

old	**vieux**	vyeh
adult	**adulte**	a-DEWLT
She is forty years old.	**Elle a quarante ans.**	ay-LA ka-rouw-TOUW
She is in her thirties.	**Elle a la trentaine.**	ay-LA la tawn-TAIN
She is about twenty.	**Elle a environ vingt ans.**	ay-LA awn-vee-ROH veh-TOUW
He is six years old.	**Il a six ans.**	ee-LA see-ZOUW

a beautiful girl
une belle fille
ewn bayl feey

a pretty woman
une jolie femme
ewn zhoh-LEE fam

a handsome man
un bel homme
eh bayl OHM

attractive	**séduisant *m* / séduisante *f***	say-dwee-ZOUN / say-dwee-ZOUNT
beautiful	**beau / bel *m* / belle *f***	boh / bayl / bayl
cute	**mignon *m* / mignonne *f***	mee-NYOH / mee-NYON
handsome	**beau / bel**	boh / bayl
pretty	**jolie**	zhoh-LEE
ugly	**laid *m* / laide *f***	layd / layd
unattractive	**moche**	mosh
dirty	**sale**	sal
elegant	**élégant *m* / élégante *f***	ay-lay-GOUN / ay-lay-GOUNT
fashionable	**à la mode**	a-la-MOD
neat	**soigné *m* / soignée *f***	swa-NYAY / swa-NYAY
casually dressed	**tenue décontractée**	tuh-NEW day-koh-trak-TAY
poorly dressed	**mal habillé *m* / mal habillée *f***	mal a-bee-YAY / mal a-bee-YAY
untidy	**négligé *m* / négligée *f***	nay-glee-ZHAY / nay-glee-ZHAY
well-dressed	**bien habillé *m* / bien habillée *f***	byeh a-bee-YAY / byeh a-bee-YAY

She is taller than him.	**Elle est plus grande que lui.**	ay-lay plu-ground kay-LWEE
He isn't as tall as her.	**Il n'est pas aussi grand qu'elle.**	eel nay-pa oh-SEEE groun kayl
She is of average height.	**Elle est de taille moyenne.**	ay-lay duh-TIE mwa-YAYN

very tall
très grand *m* /
très grande *f*
tray-groun / tray-ground

tall
grand *m* / grande *f*
groun / ground

quite tall
plutôt grand *m* /
plutôt grande *f*
plew-TOH groun /
plew-TOH ground

not very tall
pas très grand *m* /
pas très grande *f*
pa-TRAY groun /
pa-TRAY ground

short
petit *m* / petite *f*
puh-TEE / puh-TEET

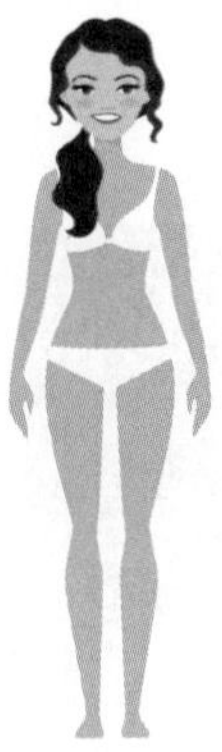

thin
mince
mehs

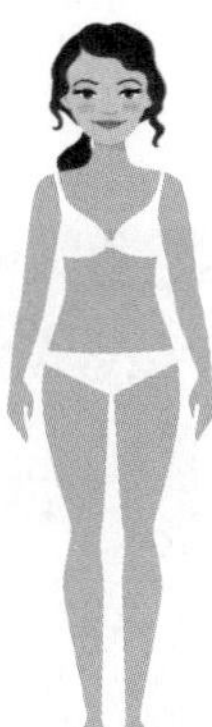

slim
svelte
svaylt

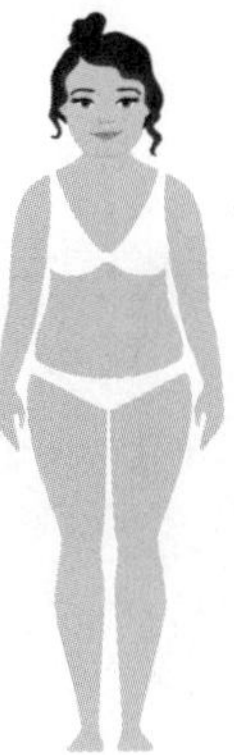

plump
rond *m* / ronde *f*
roh / rohd

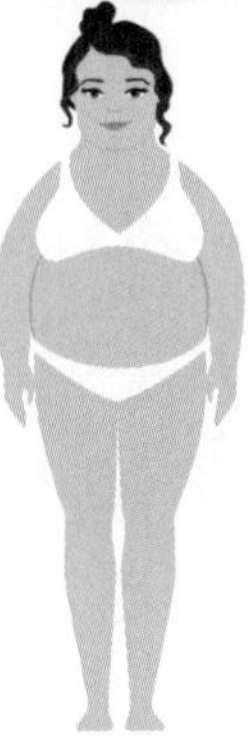

fat
gros *m* / grosse *f*
groh / grohs

slender	**élancé *m* / élancée *f***	ay-loun-SAY / ay-loun-SAY
skinny	**maigre**	maygr
obese	**obèse**	oh-BAYZ
underweight	**en sous-poids**	eh-soo-PWA
overweight	**en surpoids**	eh-sewr-PWA
She is overweight / underweight.	**Elle est trop grosse / trop maigre.**	ay-lay troh grohs / troh maygr
to lose weight	**perdre du poids**	payrdr duh-PWA

grey
gris
gree

red
roux
roo

dark
foncé
foh-CAY

black
noir
nwar

blond
blond
bloh

light
clair
klayr

chestnut
châtain
sha-TEH

brown
marron
ma-ROH

straight
droit
drwa

long
long
loh

curly
frisé
free-ZAY

short
court
koor

wavy
ondulé
oh-dew-LAY

shoulder-length
aux épaules
oh-ay-pohl

thick
épais
ay-PAY

medium-length
mi-long
mee-LOH

bald
chauve
shohv

a brunette	**une brune**	ewn-BREWN
a redhead	**une rousse**	ewn-ROOS
a blonde	**une blonde**	ewn-BLOHD
a dark-haired woman	**une femme aux cheveux foncés**	ewn-FAM oh-shuh-VEH foh-SYA
He has long dark hair.	**Il a de longs cheveux foncés.**	eel-AH duh-LOH shuh-VEH foh-SAY.
He has curly hair.	**Il a les cheveux bouclés.**	eel-AH lay-shuh-VEH boo-KLAY.
He is bald.	**Il est chauve.**	eel-AY shohv.

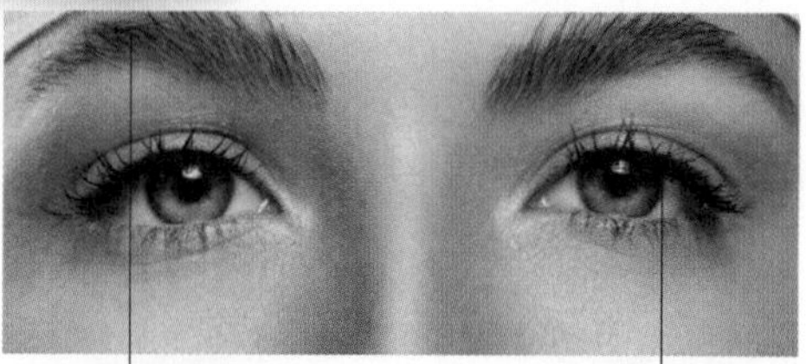

eyebrows
les sourcils
lay-soor-SEEL

eyelashes
les cils
lay-SEEL

glasses
les lunettes
lay-lew-NAYT

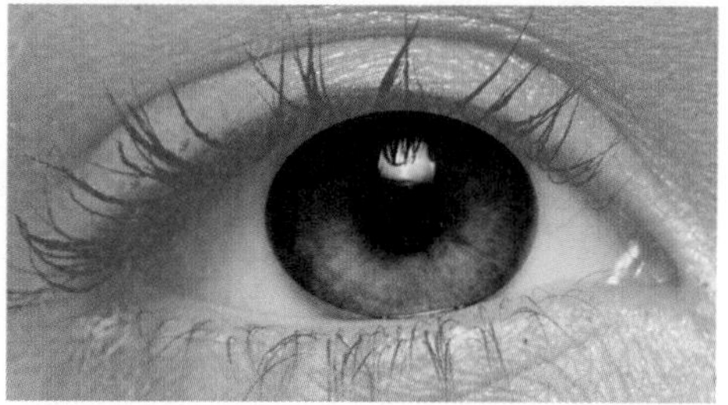

sunglasses
les lunettes de soleil
lay-lew-NAYT duh-soh-LAYY

blue	**bleu**	bleh	brown	**marron**	ma-ROH
grey	**gris**	gree	dark	**foncé**	foh-SAY
green	**vert**	vayr	light	**clair**	klayr

short sighted	**myope**	myop
blind	**aveugle**	a-VEHGL
She wears glasses.	**Elle porte des lunettes.**	ayl port day-lew-NAYT.
She has blue eyes.	**Elle a les yeux bleus.**	ay-LAH lay-ZYEH bleh.
His eyes are dark brown.	**Ses yeux sont brun foncé.**	say-ZYEH soh breh foh-SAY.

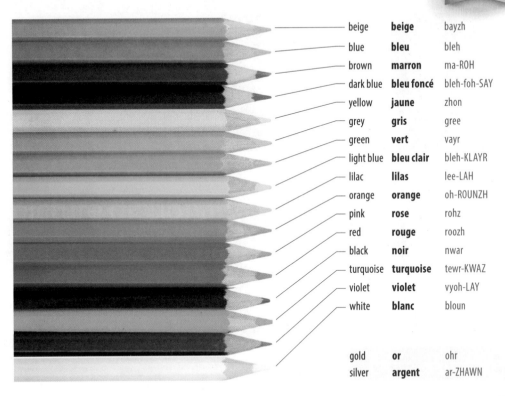

beige	**beige**	bayzh
blue	**bleu**	bleh
brown	**marron**	ma-ROH
dark blue	**bleu foncé**	bleh-foh-SAY
yellow	**jaune**	zhon
grey	**gris**	gree
green	**vert**	vayr
light blue	**bleu clair**	bleh-KLAYR
lilac	**lilas**	lee-LAH
orange	**orange**	oh-ROUNZH
pink	**rose**	rohz
red	**rouge**	roozh
black	**noir**	nwar
turquoise	**turquoise**	tewr-KWAZ
violet	**violet**	vyoh-LAY
white	**blanc**	bloun
gold	**or**	ohr
silver	**argent**	ar-ZHAWN

positive
positif
poh-see-TEEF

stubborn
têtu
tay-TEW

lucky
chanceux
shoun-SEH

dreamer
rêveur
ray-VEHR

visionary
visionnaire
vee-zyoh-NAYR

funny
drôle
drohl

talkative
bavard
bah-VAR

energetic
énergique
ay-nayr-ZHEEK

negative
négatif
nay-gah-TEEF

creative	**créatif**	cray-a-TEEF
adventurous	**aventureux**	a-vawn-tew-REH
kind	**aimable**	ay-MABL
calm	**calme**	kalm
caring	**affectueux**	a-fuh-ktew-EH
punctual	**ponctuel**	poh-ktew-AYL
crazy	**fou**	foo
frank	**franc**	froun
liar	**menteur**	mawn-TEHR
strong	**fort**	fohr

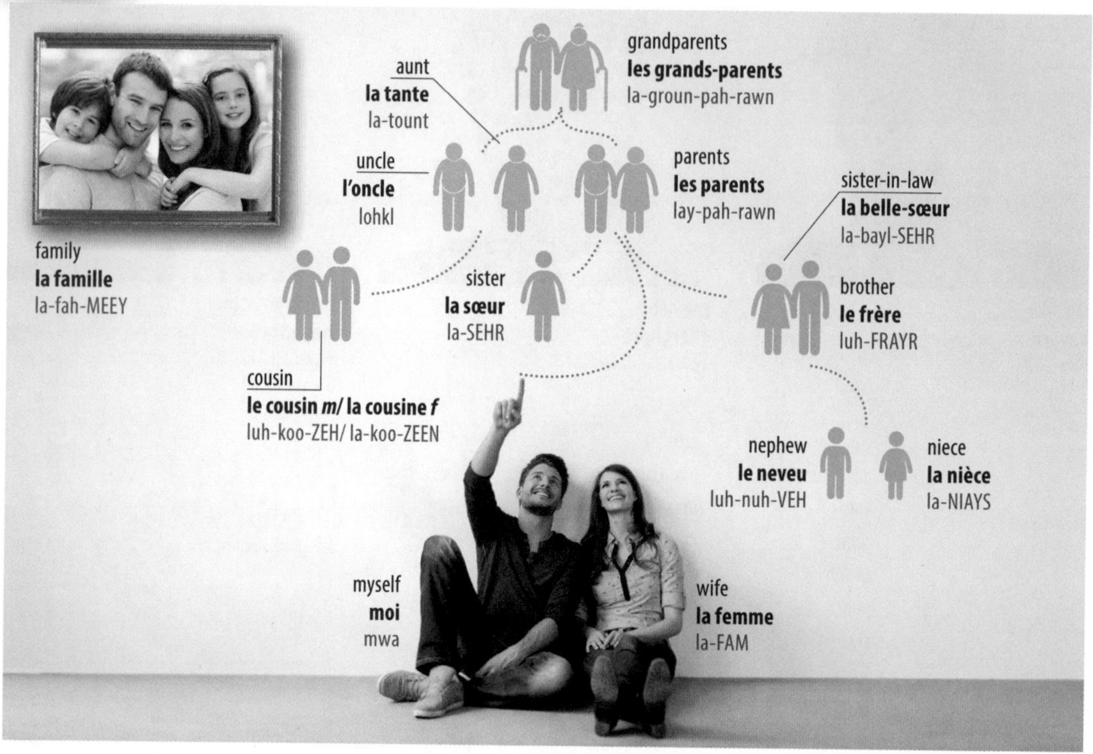

family
la famille
la-fah-MEEY

grandparents
les grands-parents
la-groun-pah-rawn

aunt
la tante
la-tount

uncle
l'oncle
lohkl

parents
les parents
lay-pah-rawn

sister-in-law
la belle-sœur
la-bayl-SEHR

sister
la sœur
la-SEHR

brother
le frère
luh-FRAYR

cousin
le cousin *m*/ la cousine *f*
luh-koo-ZEH/ la-koo-ZEEN

nephew
le neveu
luh-nuh-VEH

niece
la nièce
la-NIAYS

myself
moi
mwa

wife
la femme
la-FAM

great-grandparents	**les arrière-grands-parents**	lay-za-RYAYR-groun-pa-ROUN
husband	**le mari**	luh-ma-REE
mother	**la mère**	la-MAYR
mother-in-law	**la belle-mère**	la-bayl-MAYR
son	**le fils**	luh-FEES
twin brother	**le frère jumeau**	luh-FRAYR-jew-MOH
brother-in-law	**le beau-frère**	luh-boh-FRAYR
grandchildren	**les petits-enfants**	lay-puh-TEEeh-FOUN
daughter	**la fille**	la-FEEY
father	**le père**	luh-PAYR
father-in-law	**le beau-père**	luh-boh-PAYR
grandchild	**le petit-enfant**	luh-puh-TEE-eh-FOUN
granddaughter	**la petite-fille**	la-puh-TEET-feey
grandson	**le petit-fils**	luh-puh-TEE-fees
grandfather	**le grand-père**	luh-groun-PAYR
grandmother	**la grand-mère**	la-groun-MAYR

single child
un enfant unique
eh-nuh-FOUN ew-NEEK

family with two children
une famille avec deux enfants
ewn-fah-MEEY a-VAYK deh-zuh-FOUN

big family
une grande famille
ewn-GROUND fah-MEEY

childless
sans enfant
soun-zuh-FOUN

single father
le père célibataire
luh-PAYR say-lee-bah-TEHR

single mother
la mère célibataire
la-MAUR say-lee-bah-TEHR

adoption
l'adoption
la-doh-PSYOH

orphan
l'orphelin *m* / l'orpheline *f*
lor-fuh-LEH / lor-fuh-LEEN

widow
veuve
vehv

stepfather	**le beau-père**	luh-boh-PAYR
stepmother	**la belle-mère**	la-bayl-MAYR
to be pregnant	**être enceinte**	aytr uh-SEHT
to expect a baby	**attendre un bébé**	a-toundr eh-bay-BAY
to give birth to	**donner naissance à**	do-NAY nay-SOUNS ah
born	**né *m* / née *f***	nay / nay
to baptise	**baptiser**	bah-tee-ZAY
to raise	**élever**	ay-luh-VAY
to be engaged	**être fiancé *m* / fiancée *f***	aytr fyoun-SAY / fyoun-SAY
to marry	**se marier**	suh-ma-RYAY
to be married to	**être marié à *m* / mariée *f***	aytr ma-RYAY a / ma-RYAY
divorced	**divorcé *m* / divorcée *f***	dee-vor-SAY / dee-vor-SAY
widowed	**veuf *m* / veuve *f***	vehf / vehv
widower	**veuf**	vehf
to die	**mourir**	moo-REER

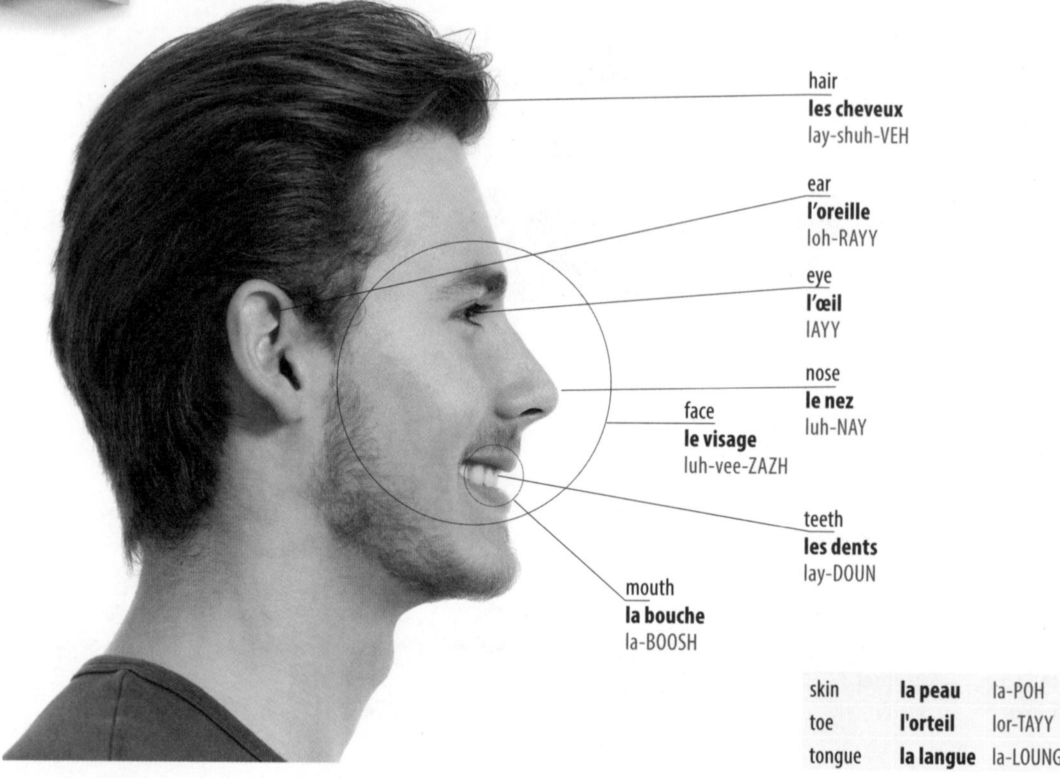

skin	**la peau**	la-POH
toe	**l'orteil**	lor-TAYY
tongue	**la langue**	la-LOUNG

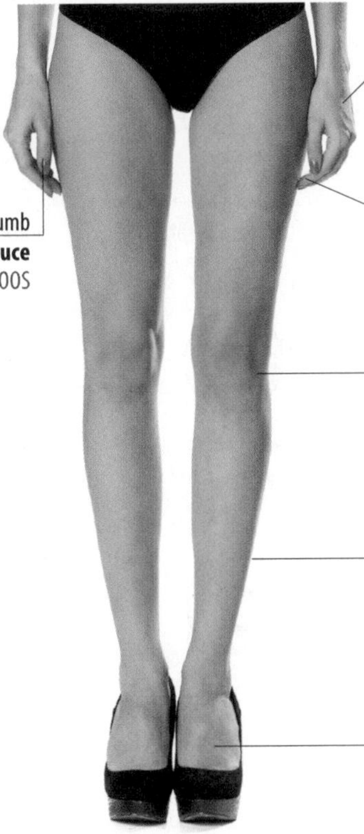

hand
la main
la-MAH
finger
le doigt
luh-DWA
thumb
le pouce
luh-POOS
knee
le genou
luh-zhuh-NOO
leg
la jambe
la-ZHAWNB
foot
le pied
luh-PYAY
head 
la tête
la-TAYT
neck
le cou
luh-KOO
shoulder
l'épaule
lay-POHL
arm
le bras
luh-BRAH
stomach
le ventre
luh-VOUNTR

angry
en colère
awn-koh-LAYR

annoyed
agacé *m* / agacée *f*
a-gah-SAY / a-gah-SAY

ashamed
honteux *m* / honteuse f
oh-TEH / oh-TEHZ

betrayed
trahi *m* / trahie *f*
trah-EE / trah-EE

confused
confus *m* / confuse *f*
koh-FEW / koh-FEWZ

confident
confiant *m* / confiante *f*
koh-FYAWN / koh-FYAWNT

cheated
floué *m* / flouée *f*
floo-AY / floo-AY

depressed
déprimé *m* / déprimée *f*
day-pree-MAY / day-pree-MAY

delighted
ravi *m* / ravie *f*
rah-VEE / rah-VEE

disappointed
déçu *m* / déçue *f*
day-SEW / day-SEW

excited
excité *m* / excitée *f*
ay-xee-TAY / ay-xee-TAY

embarrassed
gêné *m* / gênée *f*
zhuh-NAY / zhuh-NAY

furious
furieux *m* / furieuse *f*
few-RYEH / Few-RYEHZ

frightened
apeuré *m* / apeurée f
a-peh-RAY / a-peh-RAY

happy
heureux *m* / heureuse *f*
eh-REH / eh-REHZ

horrified
horrifié *m* / horrifiée *f*
oh-ree-FYAY / oh-ree-FYAY

irritated
irrité *m* / irritée *f*
ee-ree-TAY / ee-ree-TAY

intrigued
intrigué *m* / intriguée *f*
uh-tree-GAY / uh-tree-GAY

jealous
jaloux *m* / jalouse *f*
zhah-LOO / zhah-LOOZ

lazy
paresseux *m* / paresseuse *f*
pa-reh-SEH / pa-reh-SEHZ

lucky
chanceux *m* / chanceuse *f*
shoun-SEH / shaoun-SEHZ

relaxed
détendu *m* / détendue *f*
day-tawn-DEW / day-tawn-DEW

sad
triste
treest

stressed
stressé *m* / stressée *f*
struh-SAY / struh-SAY

terrified
terrifié *m* / terrifiée *f*
tuh-ree-FYAY / tuh-ree-FYA

upset
contrarié *m* / contrariée f
koh-trah-RYAY / koh-trah-RYAY

unhappy
malheureux *m* / malheureuse *f*
mah-leh-REH / mah-leh-REHZ

My hobby is ...	**Mon passe-temps est ...**	moh pas-TEH ay ...
Are you interested in ...?	**Êtes-vous intéressé par ... ?**	ayt-VOO eh-tay-ruh-SAY par ... ?

baking
la pâtisserie
la-pah-tee-SRE

coin collecting
la numismatique
la-new-mee-zma-TEEK

woodworking
le travail du bois
luh-trah-VAY duh-BWA

stamp collecting
la philatélie
la-fee-lah-tay-LEE

cooking
la cuisine
la-kwee-ZEEN

dance
la danse
la-DOUNS

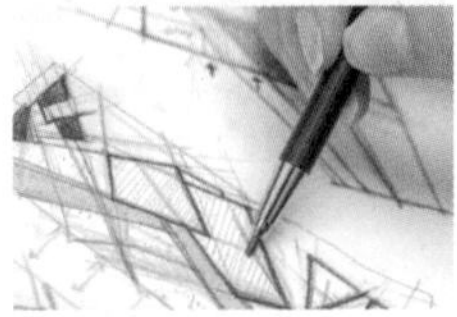

drawing
le dessin
luh-duh-SSEH

reading
la lecture
la-luhk-TEWR

jewellery making
la fabrication de bijoux
la-fa-bree-kah-SYON duh-bee-ZHOO

knitting
le tricot
luh-tree-KOH

painting
la peinture
la-peh-TEWR

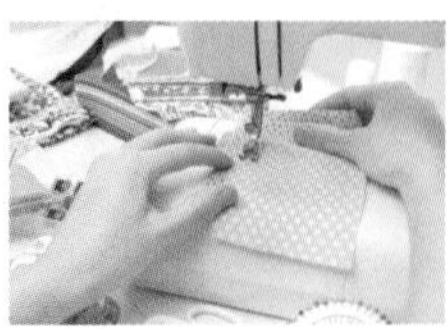

sewing
la couture
la-koo-TEWR

badminton
le badminton
luh-bad-meen-TO

bowling
le bowling
luh-boh-LEENG

boxing
la boxe
la-BOX

chess
les échecs
lay-zay-SHAYK

cycling
le vélo
luh-vay-LOH

darts
les fléchettes
lay-flay-SHAYT

diving
la plongée
la-ploh-ZHAYO

fishing
la pêche
la-PAYSH

football
le football
luh-foot-BAL

orienteering
la course d'orientation
la-koors do-ryoun-ta-SYOH

gymnastics
la gymnastique
la-zheem-nas-TEEK

handball
le handball
luh-hand-BAL

jogging
le jogging
luh-zhoh-GEENG

kayaking
le kayak
luh-kah-YAK

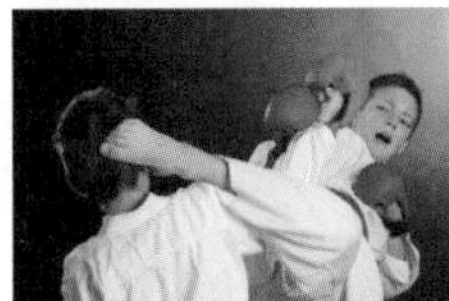

martial arts
les arts martiaux
lay-ZAR mar-SYOH

mountain biking
le VTT
luh-VAY-TAY-TAY

paintball
le paintball
luh-peh-BAL

photography
la photographie
la-foh-toh-grah-FEE

rock climbing
l'escalade
lays-ka-LAD

running
la course à pied
la-koors-a-PYAY

sailing
la voile
la-VWAL

surfing
le surf
luh-SOORF

swimming
la natation
la-na-ta-SYOH

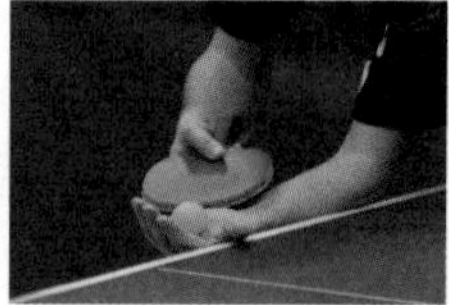

table tennis
le tennis de table
luh-tuh-NEES duh-TABL

travel
les voyages
lay-vwa-YAZH

tennis
le tennis
luh-tuh-NEES

yoga
le yoga
luh-yo-GAH

I like to swim.	**J'aime la natation.**	zhaym la-na-ta-SYON
What activities do you like to do?	**Quelles activités aimez-vous pratiquer ?**	kayl ak-tee-vee-TAY ay-MAY-voo pra-tee-KAY ?

to get up
se lever
suh-luh-VAY

to take a shower
prendre une douche
proundr ewn-DOOSH

to brush your teeth
se brosser les dents
suh-broh-SAY lay-DOUN

to floss your teeth
utiliser du fil dentaire
ew-tee-lee-SAY duh-FEEL doun-TAYR

to shave
se raser
suh-ra-ZAY

to brush your hair
se brosser les cheveux
suh-broh-SAY lay-shuh-VEH

to put on makeup
se maquiller
suh-ma-kee-YAY

to get dressed
s'habiller
sah-bee-YAY

to get undressed
se déshabiller
suh-day-za-bee-YAY

to take a bath
prendre un bain
proundr eh-BAH doun-TAYR

to go to bed
se coucher
suh-koo-SHAY

to sleep
dormir
dor-MEER

Valentine's Day
la Saint Valentin
la-SAH va-loun-TEH

graduation
la remise de diplôme
la-ruh-MEEZ duh-dee-PLOM

Easter
Pâques
pak

engagement
les fiançailles
lay-fyoun-SAIH

marriage
le mariage
luh-ma-RYAZH

bride
la mariée
la-ma-RYAY

Christmas
Noël
noh-AYL

Santa Claus / Father Christmas
le Père Noël
luh-PAYR noh-AYL

candle
la bougie
la-boo-ZHEE

decoration
la décoration
la-day-ko-ra-SYOH

mistletoe
le gui
luh-GEE

present / gift
le cadeau
luh-ka-DOH

champagne
le champagne
luh-shah-PANY

fireworks
le feu d'artifice
luh-FEH dar-tee-FEES

Advent calendar
le calendrier de l'Avent
luh-ka-loun-DRYEY

party
la fête
la-FAYT

birthday
l'anniversaire
la-nee-vuhr-SAYR

ceremony
la cérémonie
la-say-ray-moh-NEE

wedding ring
la bague de mariage
la-BAG duh-ma-RYAZH

decorated eggs
les œufs décorés
lay-ZEH day-ko-RAY

Easter Bunny
le lapin de Pâques
luh-la-PEH duh-PAK

New Year	**le Nouvel An**	luh-noo-VAYL-oun
Happy New Year!	**Bonne année !**	bon-a-NAY !
Happy Birthday!	**Joyeux anniversaire !**	zhwa-YEH a-nee-vayr-SAYR !
All the best!	**Meilleurs vœux !**	meh-YEHR veh !
Congratulations!	**Félicitations !**	fay-lee-see-ta-SYON !
Good luck!	**Bonne chance !**	bon-SHOUNS !
Merry Christmas!	**Joyeux Noël !**	zhwa-YEH noh-AYL !
Happy Easter!	**Joyeuses Pâques !**	zhwa-YEHZ PAK !

Christianity
le christianisme
luh-krees-tya-NEEZM

Confucianism
le confucianisme
luh-koh-few-sya-NEEZM

Jainism
le jainisme
luh-zhay-NEEZM

Islam
l'islam
lee-SLAM

Buddhism
le bouddhisme
luh-bood-DEEZM

Judaism
le judaïsme
luh-zhew-dah-EEZM

Hinduism
l'hindouisme
leh-doo-EEZM

Taoism
le taoïsme
luh-tah-oh-EEZM

Sikhism
le sikhisme
luh-seek-HEEZM

to confess	**se confesser**	suh-koh-fuh-SAY
without religious confession	**sans confession religieuse**	soun koh-fuh-SYON ruh-lee-GYEHZ
to believe in God	**croire en Dieu**	krwar awn-DYEH
to have faith	**avoir la foi**	a-vwar la-FWA
to pray	**prier**	pree-AY

HOME & HOUSEKEEPING

house
la maison
la-may-ZOH

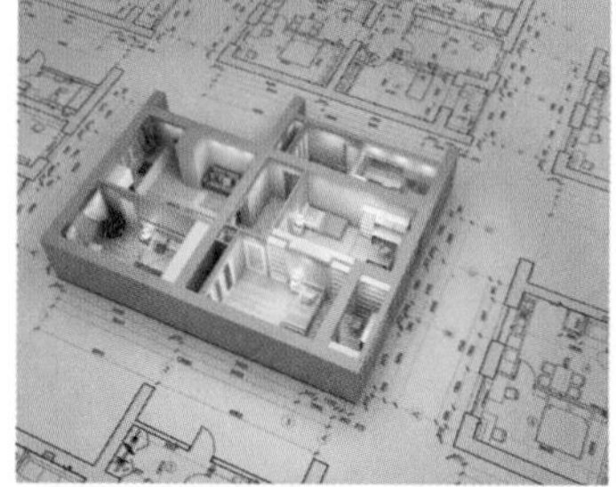

flat
l'appartement
la-par-tuh-MAWN

block of flats
l'immeuble d'habitation
lee-MEHBL dah-bee-tah-SYON

duplex / two-storey house
la maison jumelée
luh-may-ZOH zhew-muh-LAY

detached house
la maison individuelle
la-may-ZOH eh-dee-vee-dew-AYL

co-ownership
la copropriété
la-ko-proh-prya-TAY

houseboat
la péniche
la-pay-NEESH

caravan
la caravane
la-kah-rah-VAN

farm
la ferme
la-FAYRM

flatshare
la colocation
la-ko-loh-ka-SYON

Where do you live?	**Où habitez-vous ?**	oo a-bee-TAY-voo ?
I live in a flatshare.	**Je vis en colocation.**	zhuh-VEE awn-ko-lo-ka-SYON
I live with my parents.	**Je vis avec mes parents.**	zhuh-VEE a-VAYK may-pa-ROUN

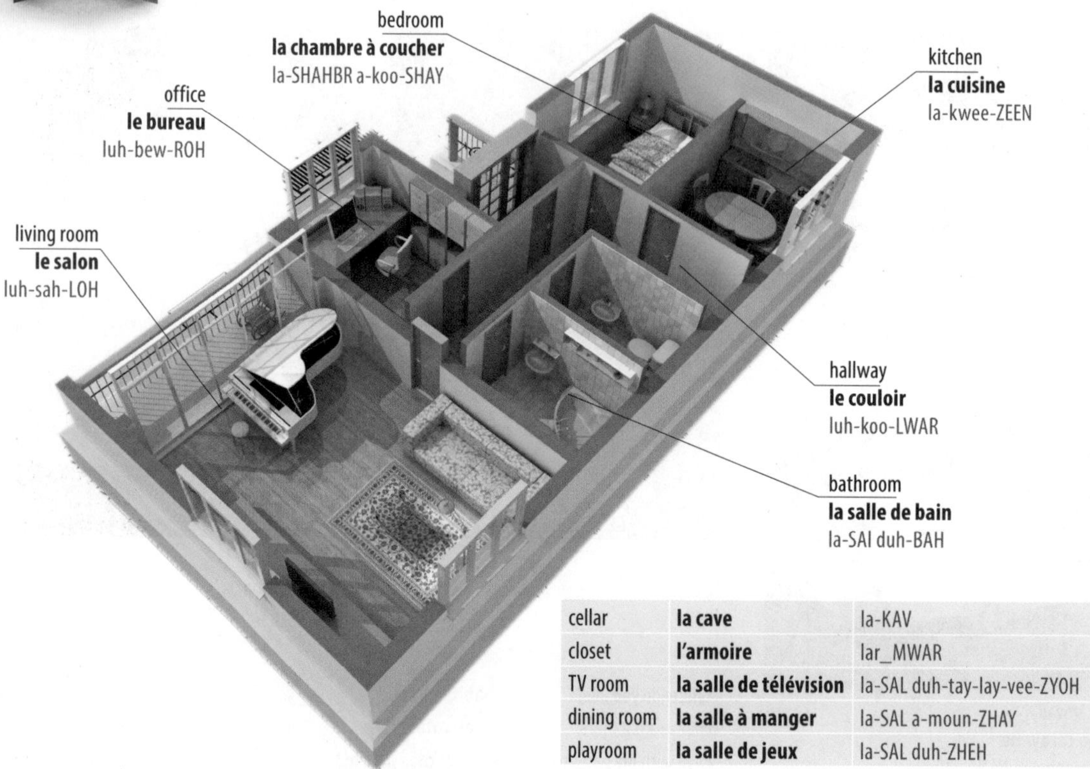

cellar	**la cave**	la-KAV
closet	**l'armoire**	lar_MWAR
TV room	**la salle de télévision**	la-SAL duh-tay-lay-vee-ZYOH
dining room	**la salle à manger**	la-SAL a-moun-ZHAY
playroom	**la salle de jeux**	la-SAL duh-ZHEH

attic
le grenier
luh-gruh-NYAY

staircase
les escaliers
lay-zays-ka-LYAY

hall
l'entrée
lawn-TRAY

garage
le garage
luh-ga-RAZH

basement
le sous-sol
luh-soo-SOL

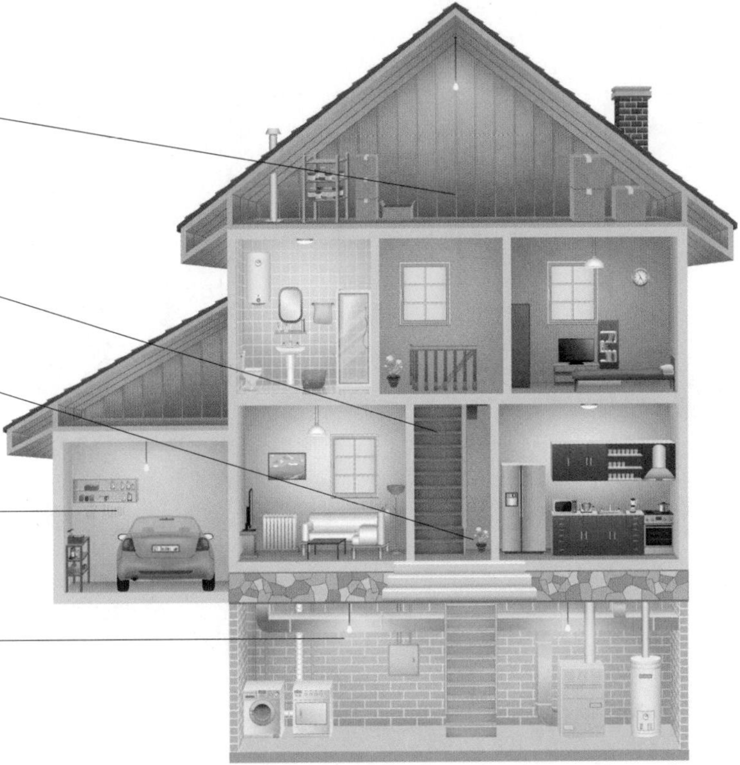

porch
le porche
luh-PORSH

patio
la terrasse
la-tuh-RAS

workshop
l'atelier
la-tuh-LYAY

window
la fenêtre
la-fuh-NAYTR

bed
le lit
luh-LEE

lamp
la lampe
la-LAHP

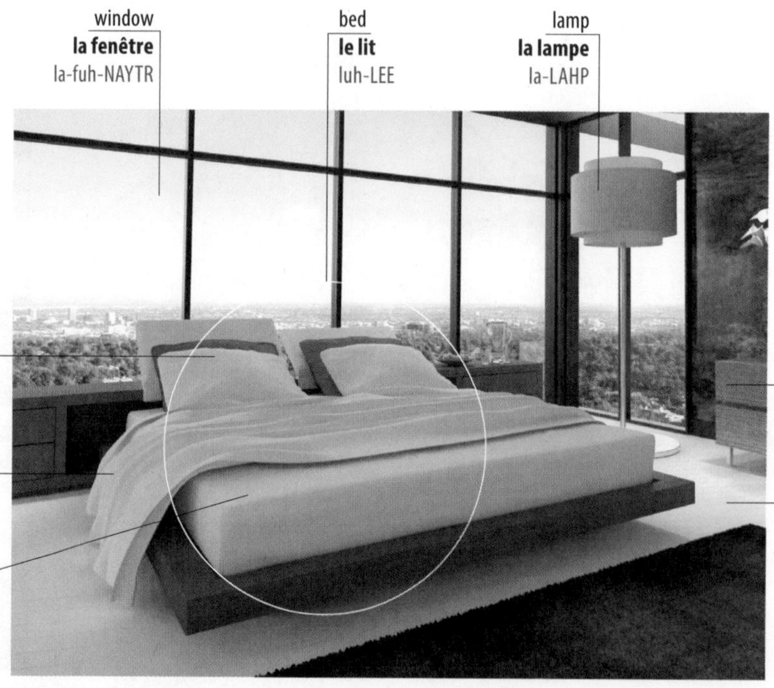

pillow
l'oreiller
lo-ray-YAY

blanket
la couverture
la-koo-vayr-TEWR

bedsheet
le drap
luh-DRA

chest of drawers
la commode
la-ko-MOD

carpet
la moquette
la-moh-KAYT

bedroom
la chambre à coucher
la-SHAHBR a-koo-SHAY

bed linen	**le linge de lit**	luh-LEHZH duh-LEE

toilet
les toilettes
lay-twa-LAYT

bidet
le bidet
luh-bee-DAY

mirror
le miroir
luh-mee-RWAR

tap
le robinet
luh-roh-bee-NAY

wash basin
le lavabo
luh-la-va-BOH

shower
la douche
la-DOOSH

bath towel
la serviette de bain
la-suhr-VYAYT duh-BAH

bathroom
la salle de bain
la-SAI duh-BAH

flush
la chasse d'eau
la-shas-DOW

bath	**la baignoire**	la-bay-NWAR

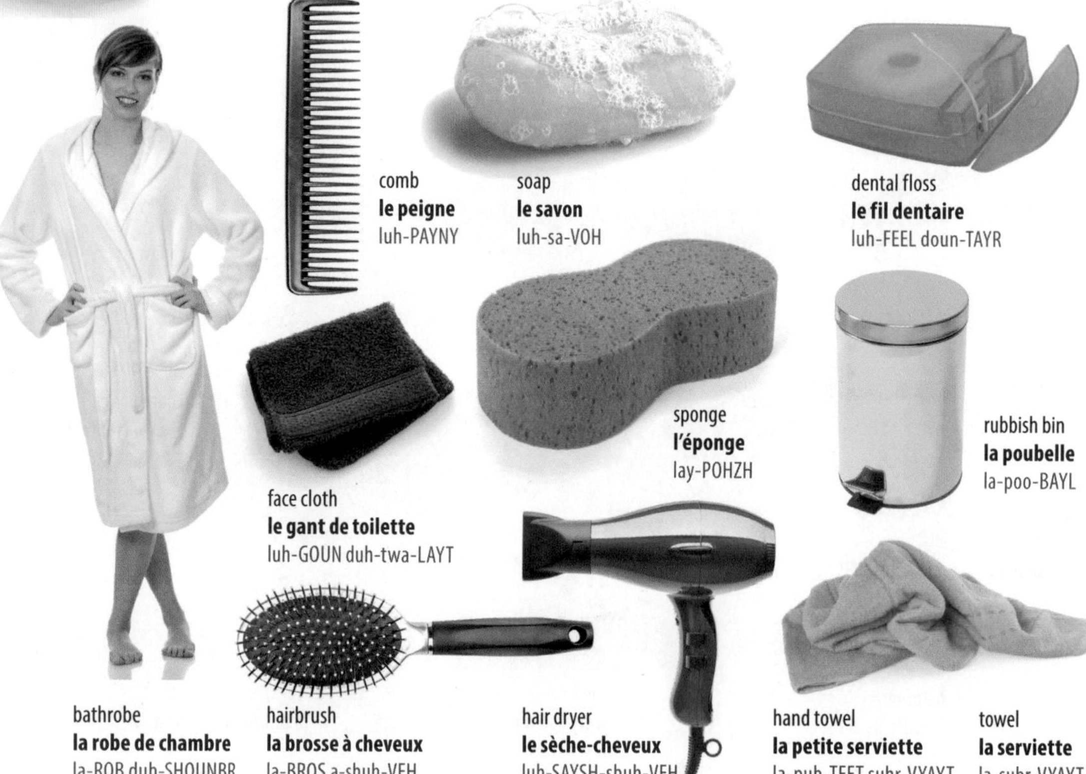

comb
le peigne
luh-PAYNY

soap
le savon
luh-sa-VOH

dental floss
le fil dentaire
luh-FEEL doun-TAYR

sponge
l'éponge
lay-POHZH

rubbish bin
la poubelle
la-poo-BAYL

face cloth
le gant de toilette
luh-GOUN duh-twa-LAYT

bathrobe
la robe de chambre
la-ROB duh-SHOUNBR

hairbrush
la brosse à cheveux
la-BROS a-shuh-VEH

hair dryer
le sèche-cheveux
luh-SAYSH-shuh-VEH

hand towel
la petite serviette
la-puh-TEET suhr-VYAYT

towel
la serviette
la-suhr-VYAYT

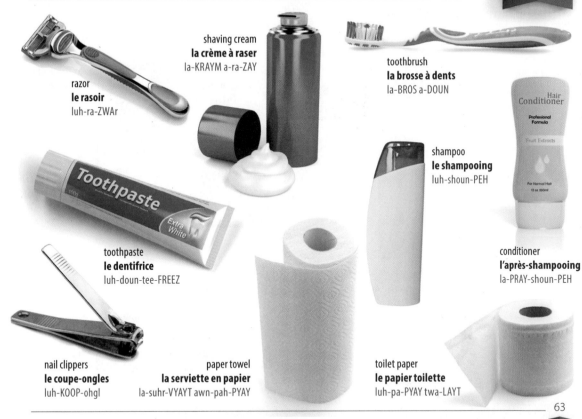

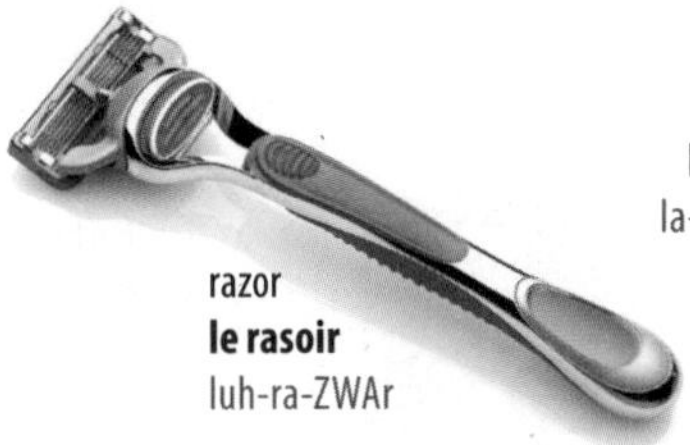

shaving cream
la crème à raser
la-KRAYM a-ra-ZAY

toothbrush
la brosse à dents
la-BROS a-DOUN

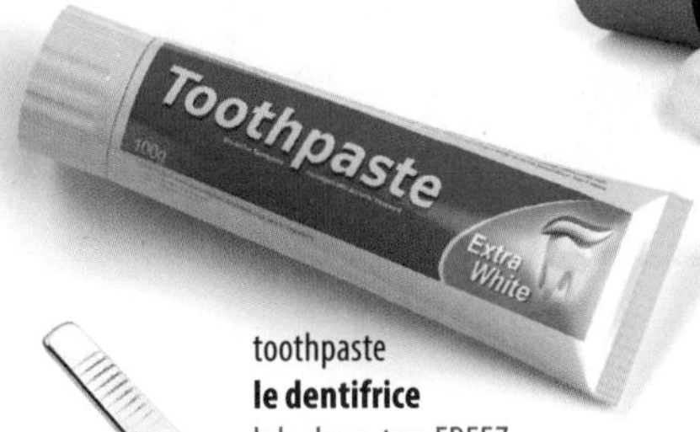

razor
le rasoir
luh-ra-ZWAr

shampoo
le shampooing
luh-shoun-PEH

toothpaste
le dentifrice
luh-doun-tee-FREEZ

conditioner
l'après-shampooing
la-PRAY-shoun-PEH

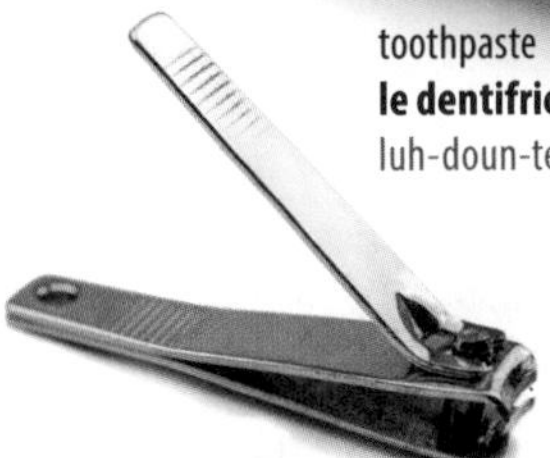

nail clippers
le coupe-ongles
luh-KOOP-ohgl

paper towel
la serviette en papier
la-suhr-VYAYT awn-pah-PYAY

toilet paper
le papier toilette
luh-pa-PYAY twa-LAYT

microwave
la micro-ondes
luh-mee-KROH-ohd
fridge
le réfrigérateur
luh-ray-free-zhay-ra-TEHR
stove
la cuisinière
la-kwee-zee-NYAYR
coffee machine
la machine à café
la-ma-SHEEN a-ka-FAY
Coffee
dishwasher
le lave-vaisselle
luh-LAV-vay-SAYL
freezer
le congélateur
luh-koh-zhay-la-TEHR
washing machine
la machine à laver
la-ma-SHEEN a-la-VAY
oven
le four
luh-FOOR
kettle
la bouilloire
la-booy-WAR
toaster
le grille-pain
luh-GREEY-peh

cookery book
le livre de cuisine
luh-LEEVR duh-kwee-ZEEN

dishcloth
la lingette vaisselle
la-leh-ZHAYT vay-SAYL

draining board
l'égouttoir
lay-goo-TWAR

kitchen roll
le papier absorbant
luh-pah-PYAY ab-sor-BOUN

plug
le bouchon
luh-boo-SHOH

tea towel
le torchon
luh-tor-SHOH

shelf
l'étagère
lay-tah-ZHAYR

sink
l'évier
lay-VYAY

tablecloth
la nappe
la-NAP

bottle opener
l'ouvre-bouteille
loovr-boo-TYAY

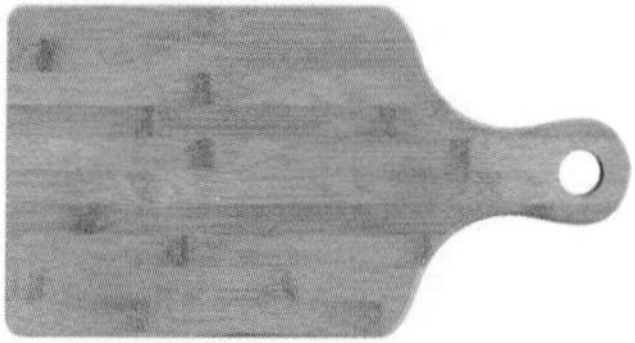

chopping board
la planche à découper
la-PLOUNSH a-day-koo-PAY

colander
la passoire
la-pa-SWAR

frying pan
la poêle
la-PWAL

grater
la râpe
la-RAP

juicer
la centrifugeuse
la-sawn-tree-few-ZHEHZ

corkscrew
le tire-bouchon
luh-TEER-boo-SHOH

kitchen scales
la balance de cuisine
la-ba-LOUNS duh-kwee-ZEEN

mixing bowl
le bol
luh-BOL

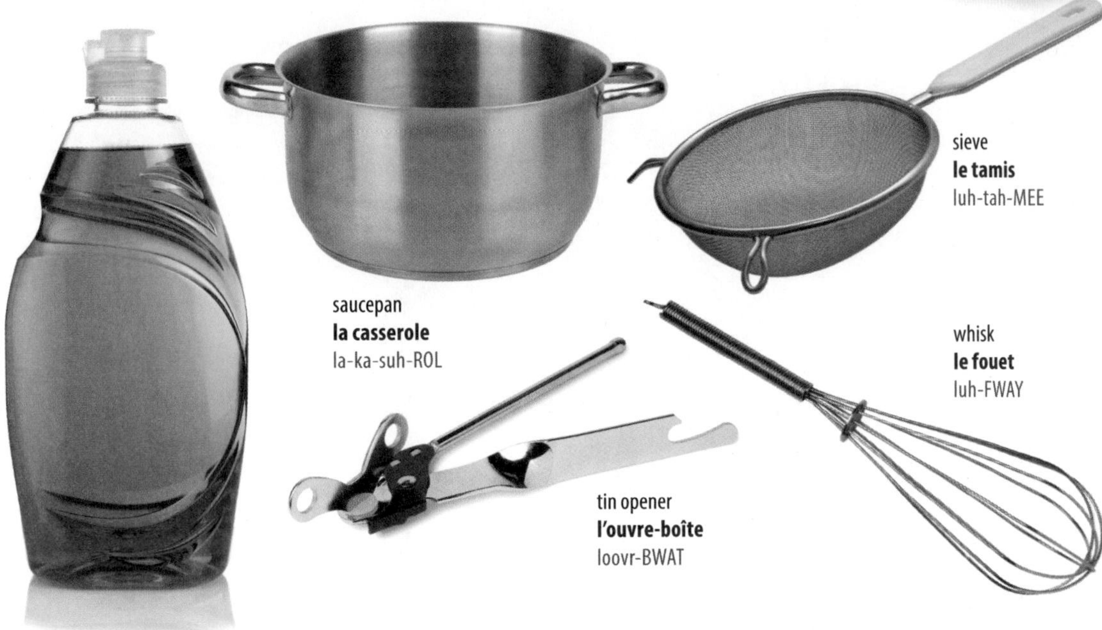

sieve
le tamis
luh-tah-MEE

saucepan
la casserole
la-ka-suh-ROL

whisk
le fouet
luh-FWAY

tin opener
l'ouvre-boîte
loovr-BWAT

washing-up liquid
le liquide vaisselle
luh-lee-KEED vay-SAYL

to do the dishes / to do the washing up	**faire la vaisselle**	fayr la-vay-SAYL
to clear the table	**nettoyer la table**	nuh-twa-AY la-TABL
to set the table	**mettre la table**	maytr la-TABL

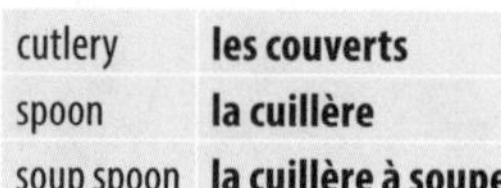

cutlery	**les couverts**	lay-koo-VAYR
spoon	**la cuillère**	la-kwee-YAYR
soup spoon	**la cuillère à soupe**	la-kwee-YAYR a-SOOP

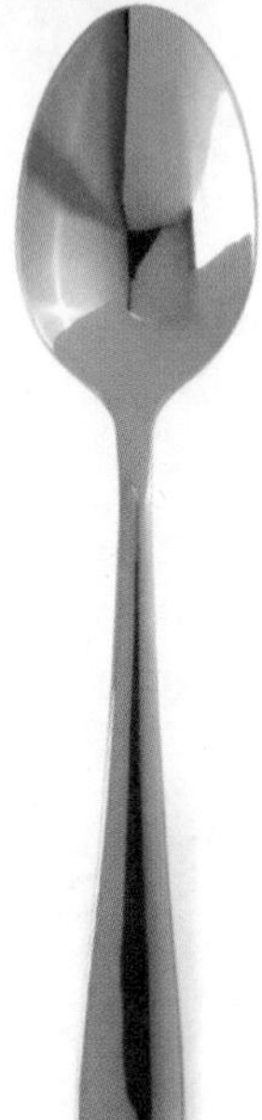

tablespoon
la cuillère de table
la-kwee-YAYR duh-TABL

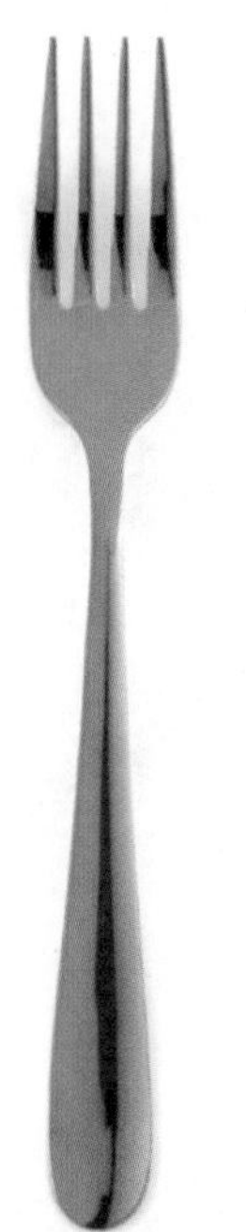

fork
la fourchette
la-foor-SHAYT

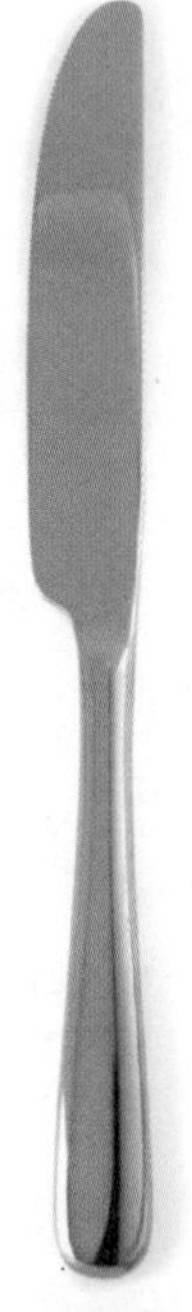

knife
le couteau
luh-koo-TOH

teaspoon
la cuillère à thé
la-kwee-YAYR a-TAY

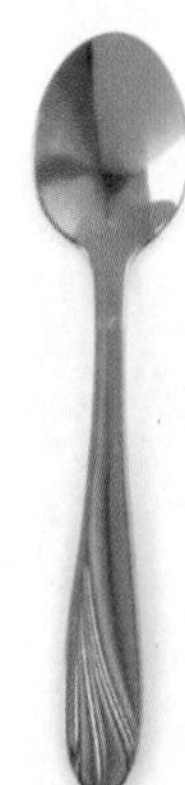

coffee spoon
la cuillère à café
la-kwee-YAYR

crockery	**la vaisselle**	la-vay-SAYL
glass	**le verre**	luh-VAYR

armchair
le fauteuil
luh-foh-TEHY

sofa
le canapé
luh-ka-na-PAY

lampshade
l'abat-jour
la-ba-ZHOOR

lamp
la lampe
la-LAHP

vase
le vase
luh-VAZ

rug
le tapis
luh-ta-PEE

bookcase
la bibliothèque
la-bee-blyoh-TAYK

shelf
l'étagère
ay-ta-ZHAYR

plant
la plante
la-PLOUNT

picture
la photo
la-foh-TOH

table
la table
la-TABL

chair
la chaise
la-SHAYZ

I can relax here.	**Je peux me détendre ici.**	zhuh-PEH muh-day-TOUNDR ee-see
Do you watch TV often?	**Regardez-vous souvent la télévision ?**	ruh-gar-DAY-voo soo-VOUN la-tay-lay-vee-ZYOH ?
What is the size of the living room?	**Quelle est la superficie de la salle à manger ?**	kay-lay la-sew-payr-fee-SEE duh-la-SAl a-moun-ZHAY ?

hair dryer
le sèche-cheveux
luh-SAYSH-shuh-VEH

iron
le fer à repasser
luh-FAYR a-ruh-pah-SAY

washing machine
la machine à laver
la machine à laver

radio
la radio
la-ra-DYO

television
la télévision
la télévision

telephone
le téléphone
luh-tay-lay-FON

cooker
la cuisinière
la-kwee-zee-NYAYR

vacuum cleaner
l'aspirateur
l'aspirateur

mobile
le portable
luh-por-TABL

microwave
le micro-ondes
luh-mee-KROH-ohd

kettle
la bouilloire
la-booy-WAR

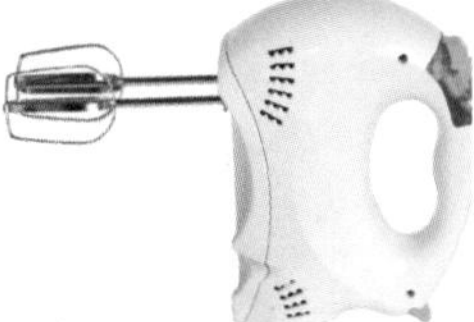

mixer
le batteur électrique
luh-ba-TEHR ay-layk-TREEK

refrigerator
le réfrigérateur
luh-ray-free-zhay-ra-TEHR

gas stove
le réchaud à gaz
luh-ray-SHOH a-GAZ

coffee grinder
le moulin à café
luh-moo-LEH a-ka-FAY

sewing machine
la machine à coudre
la-ma-SHEEN a-KOODR

razor
le rasoir
luh-ra-ZWAR

juicer
le presse-agrumes
luh-PRAYS-a-GREWM

blender
le mixeur
luh-mee-KSEHR

to clean up
nettoyer
nuh-twa-YAR

to dust
faire la poussière
fayr la-poo-SYAR

to vacuum
passer l'aspirateur
pa-SAY las-pee-ra-TEHR

to clean the windows
nettoyer les vitres
nuh-twa-YAY lay-VEETR

to clean the floor
nettoyer le sol
nuh-twa-YAY luh-SOL

to do the washing/laundry
faire la lessive
fayr la-lay-SEEV

to do the dishes
faire la vaisselle
fayr la-vay-SAYL

to make the bed
faire le lit
fayr luh-LEE

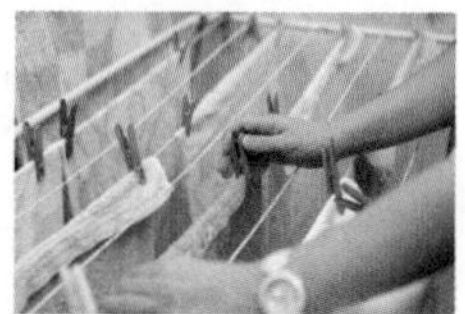

to hang up the laundry
étendre le linge
ay-TOUNDR luh-LEHZH

to iron
repasser
ruh-pa-SAY

bucket
le seau
luh-SOH

dust cloth
le chiffon
luh-shee-FOH

feather duster
le plumeau
luh-plew-MOH

dustpan
la pelle à poussière
la-PAYL a-poo-SYEHR

mop
la serpillère
la-suhr-pee-YAYR

broom
le balai
luh-ba-LAY

clothes line
la corde à linge
la-KORD a-LEHZH

peg
la pince à linge
la-PENS a-LEHZH

paper towel
le papier absorbant
luh-pa-PYAY ab-sor-BOUN

laundry basket
le panier à linge
luh-pa-NYAY a-LEHZH

scrubbing brush
la brosse à récurer
la-BROS a-ray-kew-RAY

window cleaner
le nettoyant vitres
luh-nay-twa-YOUN VEETR

sponge
l'éponge
lay-POHZG

detergent
le détergent
luh-day-tuhr-GOUN

We have to clean up.	**Nous devons faire le ménage.**	noo duh-VOH fayr luh-may-NAZH
The flat is already clean.	**L'appartement est déjà propre.**	la-par-tuh-MOUN ay day-ZHA propr
Who does the cleaning?	**Qui fait le ménage ?**	kee-FAY luh-may-NAZH ?

SCHOOL

to pass	**réussir**	ray-ew-SEE
marks	**les notes**	lay-NOT
an oral exam	**un examen oral**	eh-nay-gza-MOUN oh-RAL
a written exam	**un examen écrit**	eh-nay-gza-MOUN ay-KREE
to prepare for an exam	**préparer un examen**	pray-pa-RAY eh-nay-gza-MOUN
to repeat a year	**redoubler**	ruh-doo-BLAY

to go to school	**aller à l'école**	a-LAY a-lay-KOL
to study	**étudier**	ay-tew-DYAY
to learn	**apprendre**	a-PROUNDR
to do homework	**faire les devoirs**	fayr lay-duh-VWAR
to know	**savoir**	sa-VWAR
to take an exam	**passer un examen**	pa-SAY eh-nay-gza-MOUN

Languages
les langues étrangères
lay-LOUNG ay-troun-ZHAYR

Spanish
l'espagnol
lays-pa-NYOL

German
l'allemand
la-luh-MOUN

English
l'anglais
loun-GLAY

French
le français
luh-froun-SAY

Art
le dessin
luh-duh-SEH

Geography
la géographie
la-gay-oh-gra-FEE

Music
la musique
la-mew-ZEEK

History
l'histoire
lees-TWAR

Chemistry
la chimie
la-shee-MEE

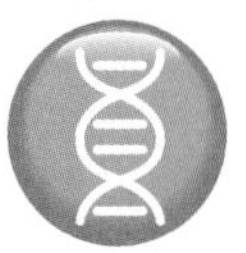

Biology
la biologie
la-byo-lo-ZHEE

Mathematics
les mathématiques
lay-ma-tay-ma-TEEK

Physical education
l'éducation physique
lay-dew-ka-SYON fee-ZEEK

scissors
les ciseaux
lay-see-ZOH

globe
le globe
luh-GLOB

school bag
le sac à dos
luh-saka-DOH

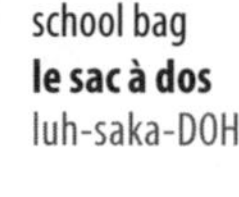

pen
le stylo
luh-stee-LOH

notebook
le cahier
luh-ka-YAY

pencil case
la trousse
la-TROOS

ruler
la règle
la-RAYGL

pencil
le crayon à papier
luh-kray-YOH a-pa-PYAY

pencil sharpener
le taille-crayon
luh-TIE-kray-YOH

rubber
la gomme
la-GOM

highlighter
le surligneur
luh-sewr-lee-NYEHR

book
le livre
luh-LEEVR

colouring pen
le feutre
luh-FEHTR

stapler
l'agrafeuse
la-gra-FEHZ

WORK

job interview
l'entretien d'embauche
leh-tray-TYEH dah-BOSH

candidate
le candidat *m* /
la candidate *f*
luh-koun-dee-DA /
la-koun-dee-DAT

application letter
la lettre de candidature
la-LAYTR duh-koun-dee-da-TEWR

recruiter
le recruteur *m* /
la recruteuse *f*
luh-ruh-krew-TEHR /
la-ruh-krew-TEHZ

CV
le CV
luh-SAY-VAY

job advertisement	**l'offre d'emploi**	lofr dah-PLWA
application	**la demande d'emploi**	la-duh-MOUND dah-PLWA
company	**la société**	la-soh-syay-TAY
education	**la formation**	la-for-ma-SYON
interview	**l'entretien**	leh-tray-TYEH
job	**le poste**	luh-POST

salary	**le salaire**	luh-sa-LAYR
gross	**brut**	brewt
net	**net**	nayt
vacancy	**le poste à pourvoir**	luh-POST a-poor-VWAR
work	**le travail**	luh-tra-VAY
to hire	**engager**	awn-ga-ZHAY
to fire	**renvoyer**	reh-vwa-YAY

assessment	**l'évaluation**	lay-va-lew-a-SYON
bonus	**la prime**	la-PREEM
employer	**l'employeur**	leh-plwa-YEHR
experience	**l'expérience professionnelle**	lex-pay-RYEHS pro-fay-syo-NAYL
fringe benefits	**les avantages sociaux**	lay-za-voun-TAZH
maternity leave	**le congé maternité**	luh-koh-ZHAY ma-tayr-nee-TAY
notice	**le préavis**	luh-pray-a-VEE
staff	**le personnel**	luh-payr-soh-NAYL
human resources officer	**l'agent des resources humaines**	la-ZHOUN day-ruh-SOORS ew-MAYN
promotion	**la promotion**	la-pro-mo-SYOH
prospects	**les perspectives d'emploi**	lay-payr-spayk-TEEV deh-PLWA
to apply for	**poser sa candidature**	po-ZAY sa-koun-dee-da-TEWR
to resign	**démissioner**	day-mee-syoh-NAY
to retire	**prendre sa retraite**	proundr sa-ruh-TRAYT
sick leave	**le congé maladie**	luh-koh-ZHAY ma-la-DEE
strike	**la grève**	la-GRAYV
trainee	**le stagiaire**	luh-sta-ZHYEHR
training course	**le stage de formation**	luh-STAZH duh-for-ma-SYON
unemployment benefits	**les prestations de chômage**	lay-prays-ta-SYON duh-shoh-MAZH
workplace	**le lieu de travail**	luh-LYEH duh-tra-VAY

employee
l'employé
leh-plwa-YAY

actor
l'acteur *m* /
l'actrice *f*
lak-TEHR /
lak-TREES

baker
le boulanger *m* /
la boulangère *f*
luh-boo-loun-ZHAY /
la-boo-loun-ZHAYR

banker
le banquier *m* /
la banquière *f*
luh-boun-KYAY /
la-boun-KYAYR

butcher
le boucher *m* /
la bouchère *f*
luh-boo-SHAY /
la-boo-SHAYR

carpenter
le charpentier *m* /
la charpentière *f*
luh-shar-poun-TYAY /
la-shar-pou-TYAYR

chef
le cuisinier *m* /
la cuisinière *f*
luh-kwee-zee-NYAY /
la-kwee-zee-NYAYR

doctor
le médecin *m* /
la médecin *f*
luh-mayd-SEH /
la-mayd-SEH

farmer
le fermier *m* /
la fermière *f*
luh-fuhr-MYEHR /
la-fuhr-MYAYR

fisherman
le pêcheur *m* /
la pêcheuse *f*
luh-pay-SHEHR /
la-pay-SHEHZ

firefighter
le pompier *m* /
la pompière *f*
luh-poh-PYAY /
la-poh-PYAYR

musician
le musicien *m* /
la musicienne *f*
luh-mew-see-SYEH /
la-mew-see-SYAYN

lawyer
l'avocat *m* /
l'avocate *f*
la-vo-KA /
la-vo-KAT

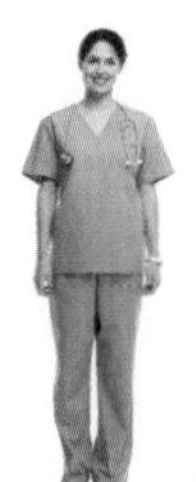

nurse
l'infirmier *m* /
l'infirmière *f*
leh-fayr-MYAY /
leh-fayr-MYAYR

pilot
le pilote *m* /
la pilote *f*
luh-pee-LOT /
la-pee-LOT

policeman
le policier *m* /
la policière *f*
luh-poh-lee-SYEH /
la-poh-lee-SYEHR

coach
l'entraîneur *m* /
l'entraîneuse *f*
leh-tray-NEHR /
leh-tray-NEHZ

sailor
le marin *m* /
la femme marin *f*
luh-ma-REH /
la-FAM ma-REH

soldier
le soldat *m* /
la femme soldat *f*
luh-sol-DA /
la-FAM sol-DA

teacher
l'enseignant *m* /
l'enseignante *f*
lawn-say-NYOUN /
Lawn-say-NYOUNT

judge
le juge *m* /
la juge *f*
luh-ZHEWZH /
la-zhewzh

tailor
le tailleur *m* /
la tailleuse *f*
luh-tay-YEHR /
la-tay-YEHZ

veterinarian
le vétérinaire *m* /
la vétérinaire *f*
luh-vay-tay-ree-NAYR /
la-vay-tay-ree-NAYR

waiter
le serveur *m* /
la serveuse *f*
luh-suhr-VEHR /
la-suhr-VEHZ

mechanic
le mécanicien *m* /
la mécanicienne *f*
luh-may-ka-nee-SYEH /
la-may-ka-nee-SYAYN

engineer
l'ingénieur *m* /
l'ingénieure *f*
leh-zhay-NYEHR /
leh-zhay-NYEHR

professor
le professeur *m* /
la professeur *f*
luh-proh-fuh-SEHR /
la-proh-fuh-SEHR

politician
le politicien *m* /
la politicienne *f*
luh-poh-lee-tee-SYEH /
la-poh-lee-tee-SYEHN

accountant	**le comptable *m* / la comptable *f***	luh-koh-TABL / la-koh-TABL
barber	**le barbier**	luh-bar-BYAY
beautician	**l'esthéticien *m* / l'esthéticienne *f***	lays-tay-tee-SYEH / lays-tay-tee-SYAYN
broker	**le courtier *m* / la courtière *f***	luh-koor-TYAY / la-koor-TYAYR
driver	**le conducteur *m* / la conductrice *f***	luh-koh-dewk-TEHR / la koh-dewk-TREES
craftsman	**l'artisan *m* / l'artisane *f***	lar-tee-ZOUN / lar-tee-ZAN
dentist	**le dentiste *m* / la dentiste *f***	luh-doun-TEEST / la-doun-TEEST
pharmacist	**le pharmacien *m* / la pharmacienne *f***	luh-far-ma-SYEH / la-far-ma-SYAYN
writer	**l'écrivain *m* / l'écrivaine *f***	lay-kree-VEH / lay-kree-VEHN
salesman	**le vendeur *m* / la vendeuse f**	luh-voun-DEHR / la-voun-DEHZ
shoemaker	**le cordonnier *m* / la cordonnière *f***	luh-kor-do-NYAY / la-kor-do-NYAYR
watchmaker	**l'horloger *m* / l'horlogère *f***	lor-loh-ZHAY / Lor-loh-ZHAYR
What's your occupation?	**Quelle est votre profession ?**	kay-LAY votr poh-fuh-SYOH ?
I work as a secretary.	**Je suis secrétaire.**	zhuh swee suh-kray-TAYR
I am a teacher.	**Je suis enseignant *m* / enseignante *f*.**	zhuh swee oun-say-NYOUN / oun-say-NYOUNT

office
le bureau
luh-bew-ROH

desk
le bureau
luh-bew-ROH

computer
l'ordinateur
lor-dee-na-TEHR

printer
l'imprimante
leh-pree-MOUNT

drawer
le tiroir
luh-tee-RWAR

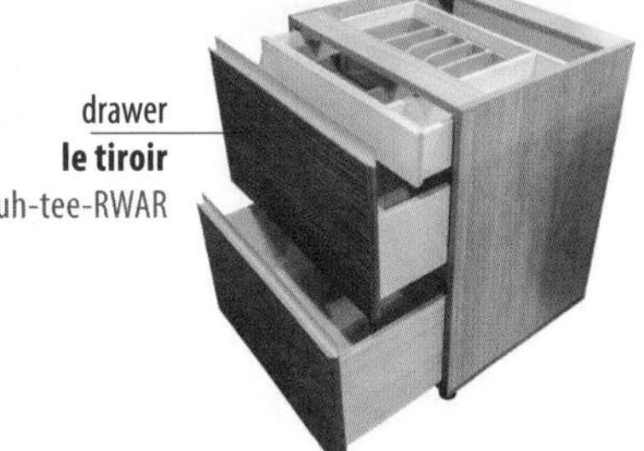

filing cabinet
le classeur à tiroirs
luh-kla-SEHR a-tee-RWAR

swivel chair
la chaise pivotante
la-SHAYZ pee-voh-TOUNT

rubber stamp
le tampon
luh-tawn-POH

telephone
le téléphone
luh-tay-lay-FON

ink pad
le tampon encreur
luh-tah-POH awn-KREHR

bin
la poubelle
la-poo-BAY

keyboard
le clavier
luh-kla-VYAY

clipboard	**le porte-bloc**	luh-PORT-blok
file	**le fichier / le dossier**	luh-fee-SHYAY / luh-doh-SYAY
in-tray	**la corbeille pour courier courant**	la-kor-BAYY poor koo-RYAY koo-ROUN
to photocopy	**photocopier**	foh-toh-koh-PYAY
to print	**imprimer**	eh-pree-MAY

bulldog clip
la pince à dessin
la-PEHS a-duh-SEH

calculator
la calculatrice
la-kal-kew-la-TREES

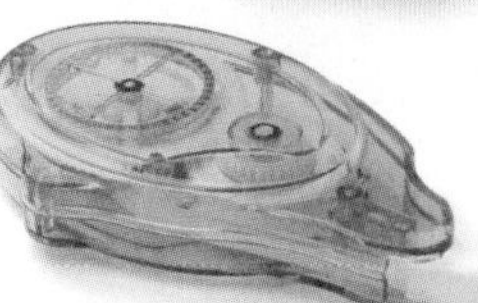

correction tape
le ruban correcteur
luh-rew-BOUN ko-ruhk-TEHR

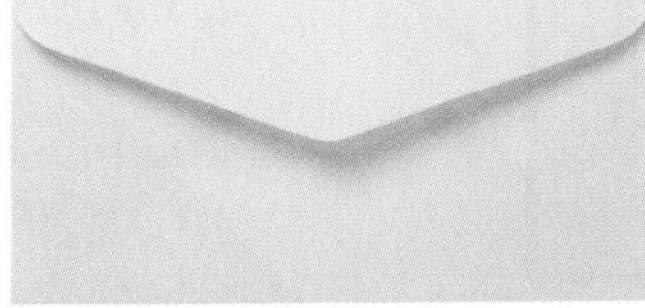

envelope
l'enveloppe
lawn-vuh-LOP

laptop
le portable
luh-por-TABL

highlighter
le surligneur
luh-sewr-lee-NYEHR

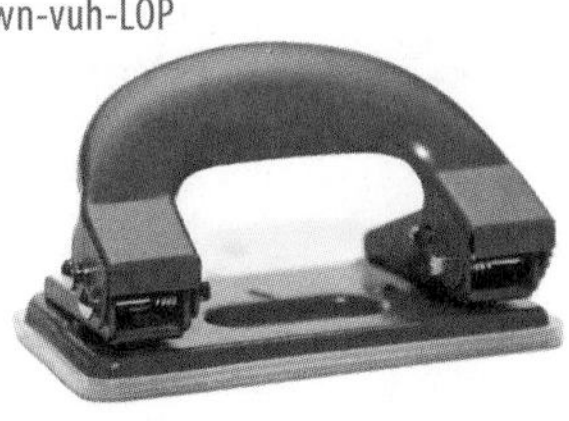

holepunch
la perforatrice
la-payr-foh-rah-TREES

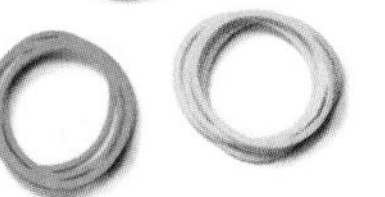

elastic bands
les élastiques
lay-zay-las-TEEK

letterhead
le papier à en-tête
luh-pa-PYAY a-eh-TAYT

notepad
le bloc-notes
luh-BLOK-not

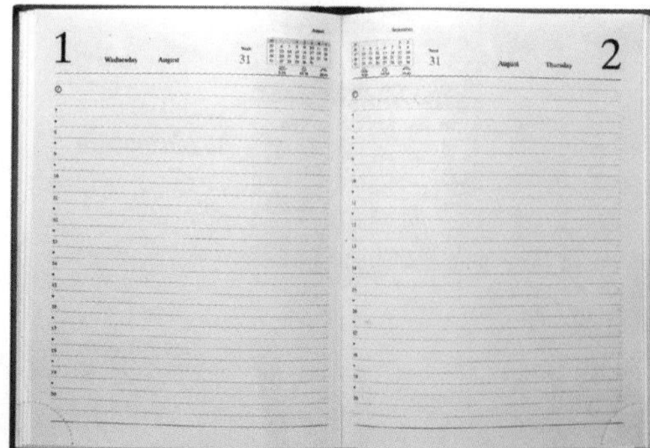

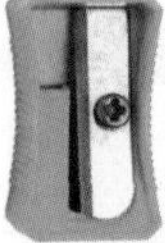

pencil sharpener
le taille-crayon
luh-TIE-kray-YOH

paper clip
le trombone
luh-troh-BON

personal organiser
l'agenda
la-zhawn-DAH

pen
le stylo
luh-stee-LOH

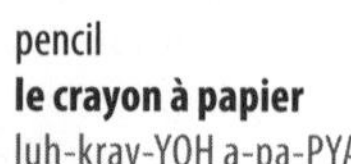

pencil
le crayon à papier
luh-kray-YOH a-pa-PYAY

sticky tape
le scotch
luh-SKOHTCH

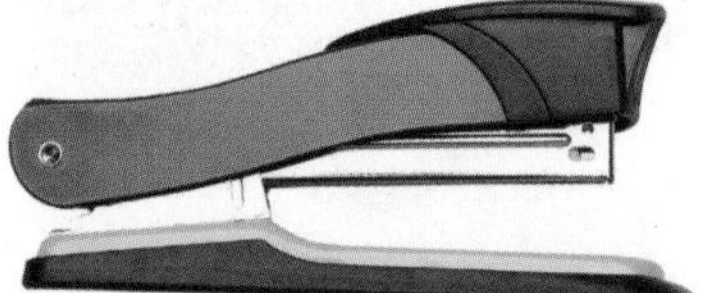

stapler
l'agrafeuse
la-gra-FEHZ

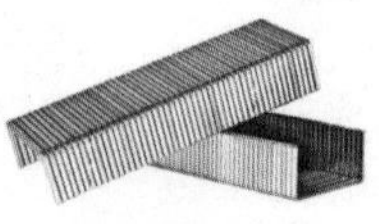

staples
les agrafes
lay-za-GRAF

FOOD AND DRINK

apple juice
le jus de pomme
luh-ZHEW duh-POM

grapefruit juice
le jus de pamplemousse
luh-ZHEW duh-pah-pluh-MOOS

orange juice
le jus d'orange
luh-ZHEW doh-ROUNZH

tomato juice
le jus de tomate
luh-ZHEW duh-toh-MAT

coffee
le café
luh-ka-FAY

milk
le lait
luh-LAY

tea
le thé
luh-TAY

with lemon
avec du citron
a-VAYK duh-see-TROH

water
l'eau
loh

with milk	**avec du lait**	a-VAYK duh-LAY	decaffeinated	**décaféiné**	day-ka-fay-ee-NAY
black	**noir**	nwar	fruit juice	**le jus de fruits**	luh-ZHEW duh-FRWEE

bacon
le bacon
luh-bay-KOH

banana
la banane
la-ba-NAN

berries
les fruits des bois
lay-FRWEE day-BWA

biscuit
le biscuit
luh-bees-KWEE

blueberries
les myrtilles
lay-meer-TEEY

bread
le pain
luh-PEH

jam
la confiture
la-koh-fee-TEWR

butter
le beurre
luh-BEHR

cereal
les céréales
lay-say-ray-AL

cheese
le fromage
luh-froh-MAZH

cottage cheese
le fromage cottage
luh-froh-MAZH ko-TAZH

doughnut
le donut
luh-doh-NAT

egg
l'œuf
lehf

ham
le jambon
luh-zhah-BOH

honey
le miel
luh-MYAYL

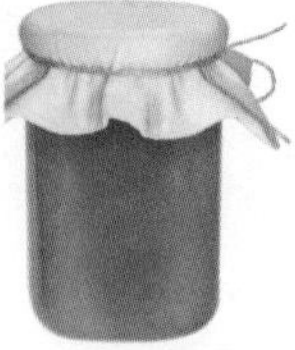

marmalade
la marmelade
la-mar-muh-LAD

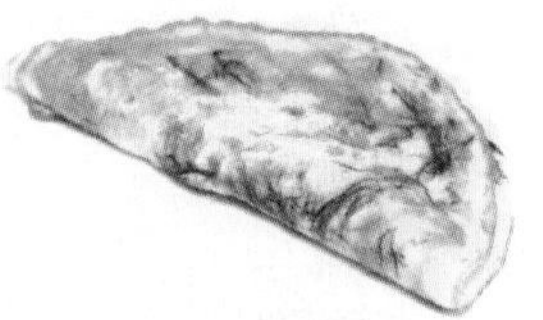

omelette
l'omelette
lom-LAYT

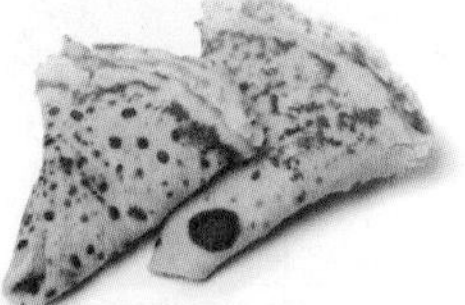

pancake
la crêpe
la-KRAYP

peanut butter
le beurre de cacahuète
luh-behr duh-ka-ka-WAYT

sandwich
le sandwich
luh-soun-DWEETCH

sausage
la saucisse
la-soh-SEES

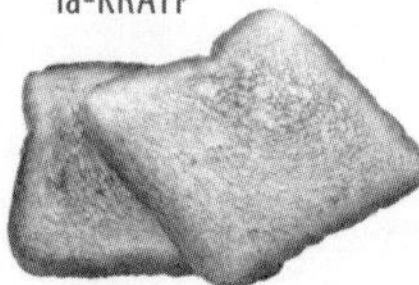

toast
le toast
luh-TOWST

waffle
la gaufre
la-GOFR

yoghurt
le yaourt
luh-yah-OORT

breakfast
le petit-déjeuner
luh-puh-TEE-day-zheh-NAY

brunch
le brunch
luh-BROUNTCH

porridge
le porridge
luh-poh-REEZH

scrambled eggs
les œufs brouillés
lay-ZEH broo-YAY

hard-boiled egg
l'œuf dur
lehf-dewr

soft-boiled egg
l'œuf à la coque
lehf-a-la-KOK

What do you eat for breakfast?	**Que mangez-vous pour le petit-déjeuner ?**	kay moun-GAY-voo poor luh-puh-TEE day-zheh-NAY ?
When do you have breakfast?	**Quand prenez-vous votre petit-déjeuner ?**	kahn pruh-NAY-voo votr puh-TEE day-zheh-NAY ?
When does breakfast start?	**A quelle heure commence le petit-déjeuner ?**	a-kay-lehr ko-mawns luh-puh-TEE day-zheh-NAY ?
What would you like to drink?	**Que voulez-vous boire ?**	keh voo-LAY-voo bwar ?
I would like a white tea.	**J'aimerais un thé au lait.**	zhay-muh-RAY eh-TAY oh-LAY

bacon
la poitrine fumée
la-pwa-TREEN few-MAY

beef
le bœuf
luh-BEHF

chicken
le poulet
luh-poo-LAY

duck
le canard
luh-ka-NARD

ham
le jambon
luh-zhah-BOH

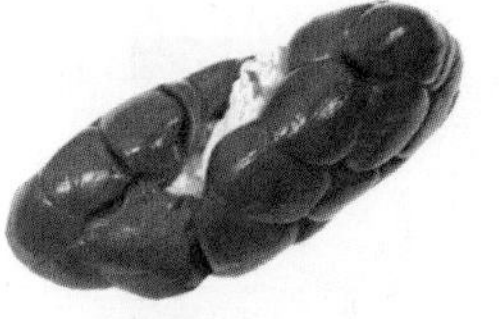

kidneys
les reins
lay-REH

lamb
l'agneau
la-NYOH

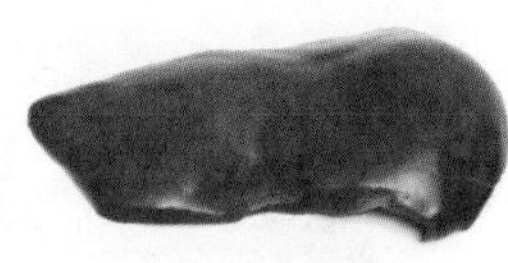

liver
le foie
luh-FWA

mince
la viande hachée
la-vyound ha-SHAY

pâté
le pâté
luh-pa-TAY

salami
le salami
luh-sa-la-MEE

meat
la viande
la-VYOUND

rabbit
le lapin
luh-la-PEH

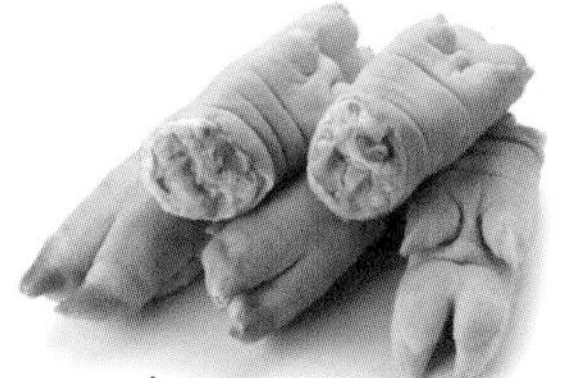

pork
le porc
luh-POR

sausage
la saucisse
la-soh-SEES

turkey
la dinde
la-DEHD

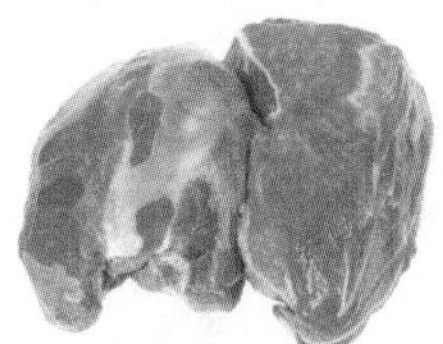

veal
le veau
luh-VOH

fruits
les fruits
lay-FRWEE

apple
la pomme
la-POM

apricot
l'abricot
la-BREE-KOH

banana
la banane
la-ba-NAN

blackberry
la mûre
la-MEWR

blackcurrant
le cassis
luh-ka-SEES

blueberry
la myrtille
la-meer-TEEY

cherry
la cerise
la-suh-REEZ

coconut
la noix de coco
la-NWA duh-ko-KOH

fig
la figue
la-FEEG

grape
le raisin
luh-ray-ZEH

grapefruit
le pamplemousse
luh-pah-pluh-MOOS

kiwi fruit
le kiwi
luh-kee-WEE

lemon
le citron
luh-see-TROH

lime
le citron vert
luh-see-TROH vayr

mango
la mangue
la-MOUNG

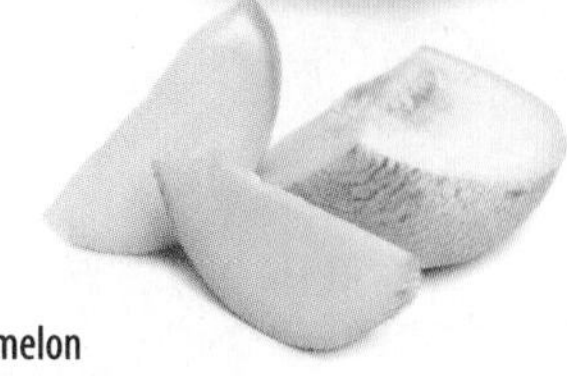

melon
le melon
luh-muh-LOH

orange
l'orange
loh-ROUNZH

peach
la pêche
la-PAYSH

pear
la poire
la-PWAR

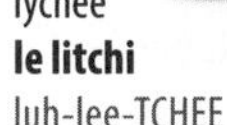

lychee
le litchi
luh-lee-TCHEE

clementine
la clémentine
la-klay-mawn-TEEN

papaya
la papaye
la-pa-PAY

pineapple
l'ananas
la-na-NAH

kumqvat
le kumquat
luh-koom-KAT

raspberry
la framboise
la-frah-BWAZ

plum
la prune
la-PREWN

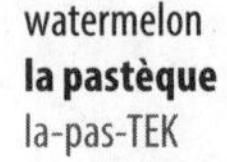

watermelon
la pastèque
la-pas-TEK

nectarine
la nectarine
la-nayk-ta-REEN

persimmon
le kaki
luh-ka-KEE

redcurrant
la groseille
la-groh-ZAYY

rhubarb
la rhubarbe
la-REW-BARB

pomegranate
la grenade
la-gruh-NAD

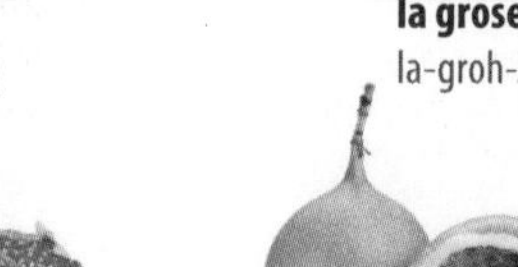

strawberry
la fraise
la-FRAYZ

passion fruit
le fruit de la passion
luh-FRWEE duh-la-pa-SYON

vegetables
les légumes
lay-lay-GEWM

artichoke
l'artichaut
lar-tee-SHOH

asparagus
l'asperge
las-PAYRZH

avocado
l'avocat
la-voh-KAH

beansprouts
les germes de soja
lay-ZHAYRM duh-soh-ZHAH

beetroot
la betterave
la-buh-TRAV

broccoli
le brocoli
luh-bro-koh-LEE

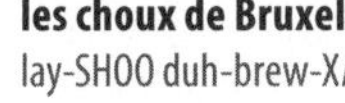

Brussels sprouts
les choux de Bruxelles
lay-SHOO duh-brew-XAYL

cabbage
le chou
luh-SHOO

aubergine
l'aubergine
loh-bayr-ZHEEN

carrot
la carotte
la-ka-ROT

cauliflower
le chou-fleur
luh-shoo-FLEHR

celery
le céleri
luh-say-luh-REE

courgette
la courgette
la-koor-ZHAYT

cucumber
le concombre
luh-koh-KOHBR

garlic
l'ail
lie

ginger
le gingembre
luh-zheh-ZHAHBR

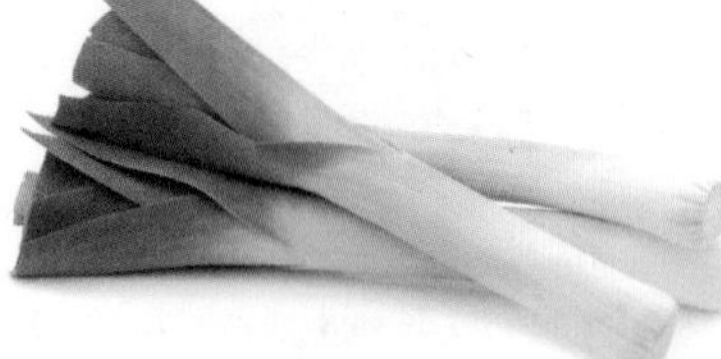

leek
le poireau
luh-pwa-ROH

lettuce
la salade verte
la-sa-LAD vayrt

mushroom
le champignon
luh-shoun-pee-NYOH

onion
l'oignon
lo-NYOH

peas
les petits pois
lay-puh-TEE pwa

potato
la pomme de terre
la-POM duh-TAYR

pumpkin
la citrouille
la-see-TROOY

spinach
les épinards
lay-zay-pee-NAR

radish
le radis
luh-ra-DEE

sweetcorn
le maïs
luh-ma-EES

tomato
la tomate
la-toh-MAT

spring onion
l'oignon vert
lo-NYOH vayr

red pepper
le poivron rouge
luh-pwa-VROH roozh

green beans
les haricots verts
lay-a-ree-KO vayr

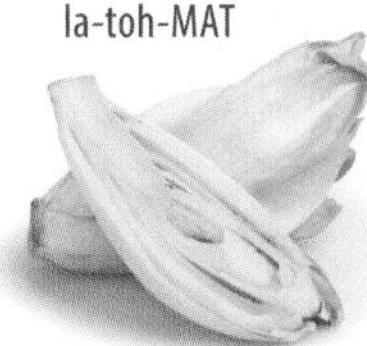

chicory
l'endive
lah-DEEV

turnip
le navet
luh-na-VAY

cuttlefish
la seiche
la-SAYSH

haddock
le haddock
luh-ah-DOK

lemon sole
la sole
la-SOHL

halibut
le flétan
luh-flay-TOUN

mackerel
le maquereau
luh-ma-keh-ROH

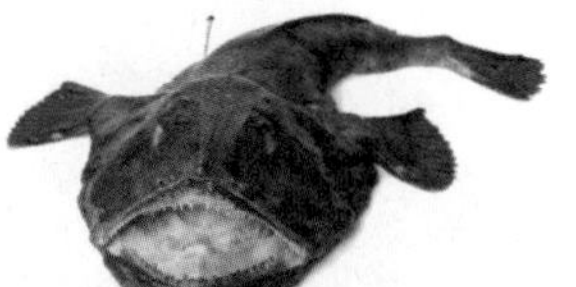

monkfish
la baudroie
la-boh-DRWA

mussels
les moules
lay-MOOL

sardine
la sardine
la-sar-DEEN

sea bass
le loup de mer
luh-LOO duh-MAYR

sea bream
la dorade
la-doh-RAD

swordfish
l'espadon
lay-spa-DOH

trout
la truite
la-TRWEET

crab
le crabe
luh-KRAB

crayfish
l'écrevisse
lay-kruh-VEES

lobster
le homard
luh-oh-MAR

tuna
le thon
luh-TOH

octopus
le poulpe
luh-POOLP

oyster
l'huître
lweetr

prawn / shrimp
la crevette
la-kruh-VAYT

scallop
la coquille Saint-Jacques
la-ko-KEEY seh-ZHAK

salmon
le saumon
luh-soh-MOH

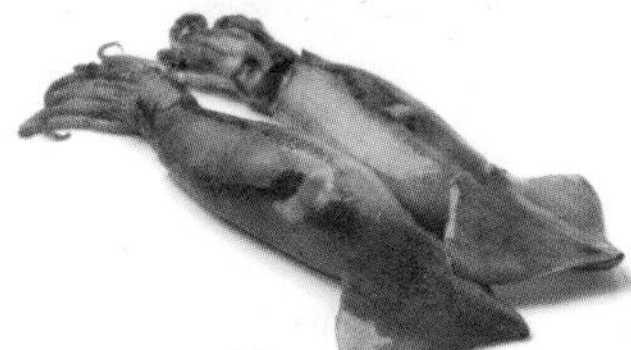

squid
le calamar
luh-kal-MAR

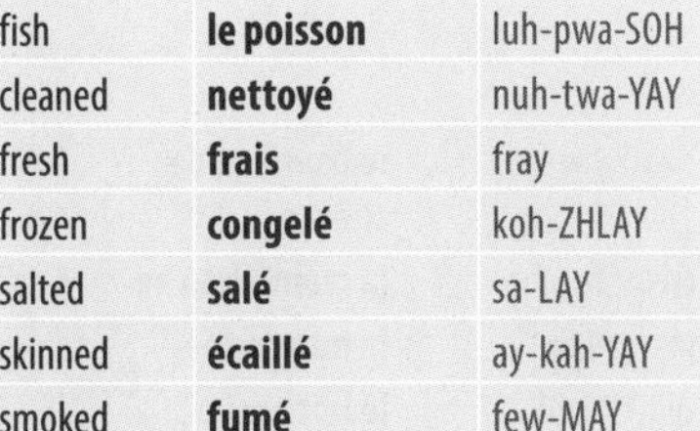

fish	**le poisson**	luh-pwa-SOH
cleaned	**nettoyé**	nuh-twa-YAY
fresh	**frais**	fray
frozen	**congelé**	koh-ZHLAY
salted	**salé**	sa-LAY
skinned	**écaillé**	ay-kah-YAY
smoked	**fumé**	few-MAY

cheese
le fromage
luh-froh-MAZH

cream
la crème
la-KRAYM

egg
l'œuf
lehf

milk
le lait
luh-LAY

cottage cheese
la faisselle
la-fay-SAYL

blue cheese
le fromage bleu
luh-froh-MAZH bleh

butter
le beurre
luh-BEHR

goat's cheese	**le fromage de chèvre**	luh-froh-MAZH duh-SHAYVR
crème fraîche	**la crème fraîche**	la-KRAYM fraysh
margarine	**la margarine**	la-mar-ga-REEN
full-fat milk	**le lait entier**	luh-LAY eh-TYAY

semi-skimmed milk	**le lait demi-écrémé**	luh-LAY duh-MEE-ay-kray-MAY
skimmed milk	**le lait écrémé**	luh-LAY ay-kray-MAY
sour cream	**la crème aigre**	la-KRAYM aygr
yoghurt	**le yaourt**	luh-yah-OORT

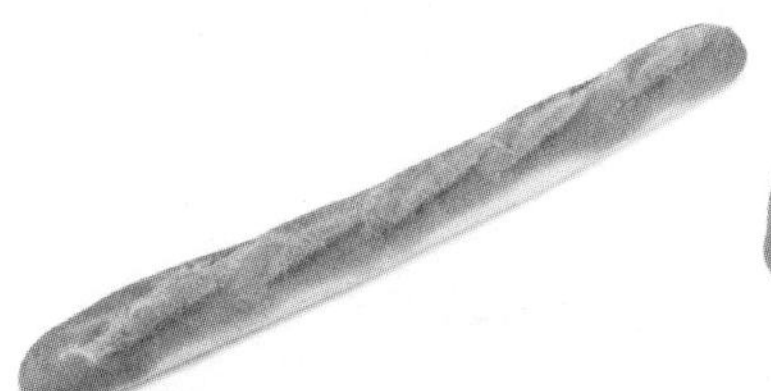

baguette
la baguette
la-ba-GAYT

bread rolls
les petits pains
lay-peh-TEE PEH

brown bread
le pain complet
luh-PEH koh-PLAY

cake
le gâteau
luh-gah-TOH

loaf
la miche
la-MEESH

white bread
le pain blanc
luh-PEH bloun

garlic bread	**le pain à l'ail**	luh-PEH a-LI	quiche	**la quiche**	la-KEESH
pastry	**la pâtisserie**	la-pah-tee-SREE	sliced loaf	**le pain en tranches**	luh-PEH oun-trounsh
pitta bread	**le pain pita**	luh-PEH pee-TAH	sponge cake	**la génoise**	la-zhay-nwaz

ketchup
le ketchup
luh-kay-TCHAP

mayonnaise
la mayonnaise
la-ma-YOH-NAYZ

mustard
la moutarde
la-moo-TARD

vinegar
le vinaigre
luh-vee-NAYGR

salt
le sel
luh-SUHL

pepper
le poivre
luh-PWAVR

basil	**le basilic**	luh-ba-zee-LEEK
chilli powder	**le piment en poudre**	luh-pee-MAWN awn-POODR
chives	**la ciboulette**	la-see-boo-LAYT
cinnamon	**la cannelle**	la-ka-NAYL
coriander	**la coriandre**	la-ko-RYOUNDR
cumin	**le cumin**	luh-kew-MAH
curry	**le curry**	luh-kew-REE
dill	**l'aneth**	la-NAYT
nutmeg	**la noix de muscade**	la-NWA duh-mews-KAD
paprika	**le paprika**	luh-pa-pree-KAH

parsley	**le persil**	luh-puhr-SEEL
rosemary	**le romarin**	luh-ro-ma-REH
saffron	**le safran**	luh-sa-FROUN
sage	**la sauge**	la-SOHZH
salad dressing	**la sauce de salade**	la-SOHS duh-sa-LAD
spices	**les épices**	lay-zay-PEES
thyme	**le thym**	luh-TEH
vinaigrette	**la vinaigrette**	la-vee-nay-GRAYT

bag
le sac
luh-SAK

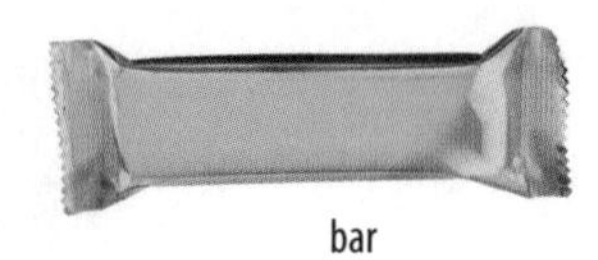

bar
la barre
la-BAR

bottle
la bouteille
la-boo-TAYY

jar
le pot
luh-POH

carton
le carton
luh-kar-TOH

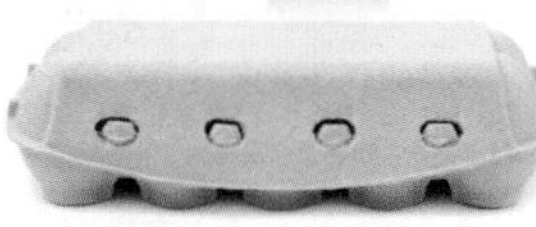

box
la boîte
la-BWAT

pack
le pack
luh-PAK

packet
le sachet
luh-sa-SHAY

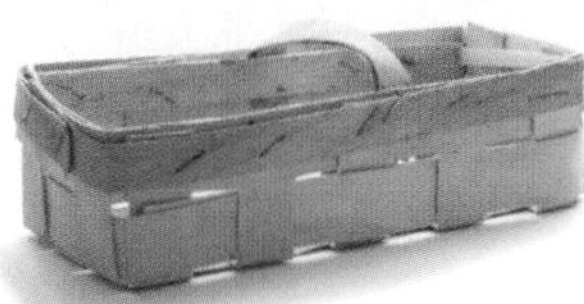

punnet
la barquette
la-bar-KAY

a bag of potatoes	**un sac de pommes de terre**	eh-SAK duh-POM-duh-TAYR
chocolate bar	**une barre de chocolat**	ewn bar duh-sho-ko-LAH
two bottles of mineral water	**deux bouteilles d'eau minérale**	deh boo-TEIY doh-mee-nay-RAL
a carton of milk	**un carton de lait**	eh-kar-TOH duh-LAY
a jar of jam	**un pot de confiture**	eh-POH duh-koh-fee-TEWR

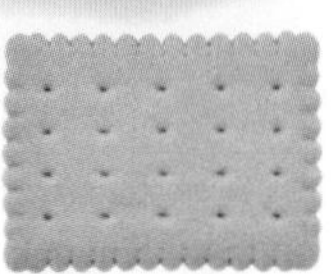
biscuit
le biscuit
luh-bees-KWEE

chocolate
le chocolat
luh-sho-ko-LA

chocolate cake
le gâteau au chocolat
luh-gah-TOH oh-sho-ko-LAH

apple pie
la tarte aux pommes
la-TART oh-POM

doughnut
le donut
luh-doh-NAT

fruit cake
le gâteau aux fruits
luh-ga-TOH oh-FRWEE

fruit salad
la salade de fruits
la-sa-LAD duh-FWREE

cheesecake
le gâteau au fromage
luh-gah-TOH oh-froh-MAZH

gingerbread
le pain d'épice
luh-PEH day-PEES

ice cream
la glace
la-GLAS

muffin
le muffin
luh-ma-FEEN

pudding
la crème dessert
la-KRAYM duh-SAYR

milkshake
le milk-shake
luh-meelk-SHEIK

marshmallow
la guimauve
la-gee-MOV

macaroon
le macaron
luh-ma-ka-ROH

waffle
la gaufre
la-GOFR

pancakes
les crêpes
lay-KRAYP

strudel
le strudel
luh-strew-DAYL

crème caramel
la crème caramel
la-KRAYM ka-ra-MAYL

honey
le miel
luh-luh-MYAYL

cake	**le gâteau**	luh-gah-TOH
coconut cake	**le gâteau à la noix de coco**	luh-gah-TOH a-la-NWA duh-ko-KOH
dessert	**le dessert**	luh-duh-SAYRT
frozen yoghurt	**le yaourt glacé**	luh-yah-OORT
rice pudding	**le riz au lait**	luh-REE oh-LAY
I like to eat sweets.	**J'aime les bonbons.**	zhaym lay-boh-BOH
I cannot eat anything sweet.	**Je ne peux pas manger de sucreries.**	zhuh nuh peh pa moun-ZHAY duh-sew-kruh-REE

cheeseburger
le cheeseburger
luh-tcheez-bewr-GAYR

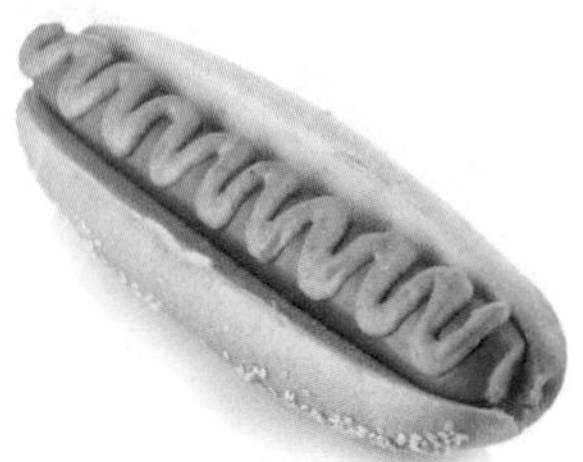

hot dog
le hot-dog
luh-oh-DOG

fish sandwich
le sandwich au poisson
luh-soun-DWEETCH oh-pwa-SOH

fried chicken
le poulet frit
luh-poo-LAY free

French fries
les frites
lay-FREET

nachos
les nachos
lay-na-TCHOH

taco
le taco
luh-ta-KOH

burrito
le burrito
luh-bew-ree-TOH

pizza
la pizza
la-pee-ZAH

hamburger
le hamburger
luh-ah-bewr-GAYR

chicken sandwich
le sandwich au poulet
luh-soun-DWEETCH oh-poo-LAY

fish and chips
le poisson-frites
luh-pwa-SOH-freet

to peel	**éplucher**	ay-plew-SHAY
to grate	**râper**	ra-PAY
to chop	**hacher**	a-SHAY
to crush	**écraser**	ay-kra-SAY
to beat	**battre**	batr
to grease	**graisser**	gra-SAY
to break	**casser**	ka-SAY
to stir	**remuer**	reh-mew-AY
to knead	**pétrir**	pay-TREER
to steam	**cuire à la vapeur**	kweer a-la-va-PEHR
to weigh	**peser**	peh-SAY
to add	**ajouter**	a-zhoo-TAY
to bake	**faire cuire**	fayr kweer
to stir-fry	**faire sauter**	fayr soh-TAY
to grill	**griller**	gree-YAY
to roast	**rôtir**	roh-TEER
to barbecue	**cuire au barbecue**	kweer oh-bar-beh-KEW
to fry	**faire frire**	fayr FREER

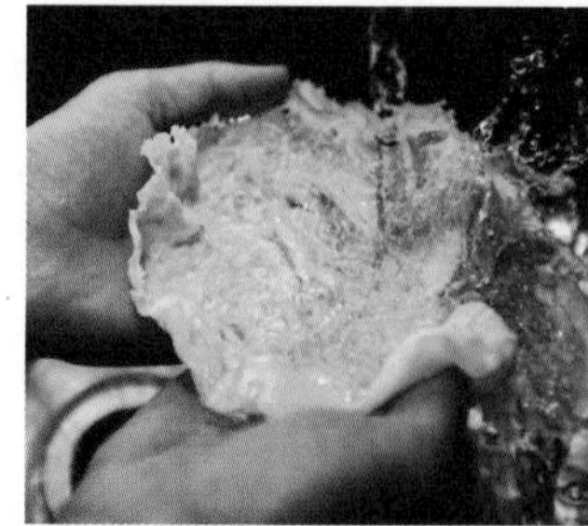

to wash
laver
la-VAY

to cut
couper
koo-PAY

to mix
mélanger
may-loun-ZHAY

to boil
bouillir
boo-YEER

bar
le bar
luh-BAR

buffet
le buffet
luh-bew-FAY

bill
l'addition
la-dee-SYOH

bistro
le bistrot
luh-bees-TROH

café
le café
luh-ka-FAY

dessert
le dessert
luh-duh-SAYR

menu
la carte
la-KART

canteen
la cantine
la-koun-TEEN

pizzeria
la pizzéria
la-pee-za-RYAH

pub
le pub
luh-PAB

salad bar
le bar à salades
luh-BAR a-sa-LAD

deli
l'épicerie fine
lay-pee-say-REE feen

self-service
le libre-service
luh-luh-LEEBR sehr-VEES

take-out / take-away
le plat à emporter
luh-PLAH a-eh-por-TAY

waiter
le serveur
luh-sehr-VEHR

waitress
la serveuse
la-sehr-VEHZ

à la carte	**à la carte**	a-la-KART
starter	**l'entrée**	leh-TRAY
booking	**la réservation**	la-ray-sehr-va-SYOH
complimentary	**gratuit**	gra-TWEE

dish	**le plat**	luh-PLAH
main course	**le plat principal**	luh-PLA preh-see-PAL
to order	**commander**	ko-moun-DAY
speciality	**la spécialité**	la-spay-sya-lee-TAY
aperitif	**l'apéritif**	la-pay-ree-TEEF

What do you want to order?	**Que voudriez-vous commander ?**	keh voo-dryay-VOO ko-moun-DAY ?
I would like to see the menu.	**Je voudrais voir la carte.**	zhuh voo-DRAY vwar la-KART
We'll take the set menu.	**Nous prendrons la formule.**	noo pawn-DROH la-for-MEWL

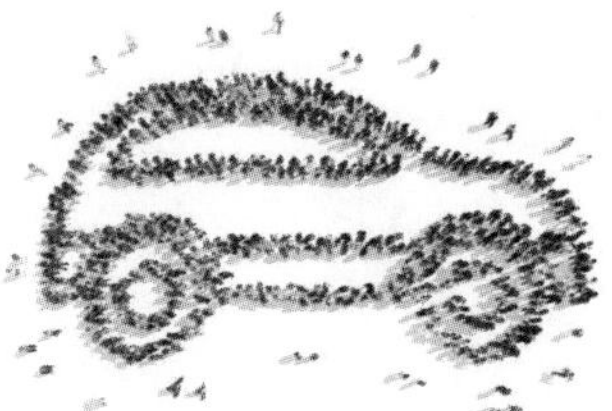

TRAVEL AND LEISURE

to travel by bus
voyager en bus
vwa-ya-ZHAY uh bews

to travel by plane
voyager en avion
vwa-ya-ZHAY uh a-VYOH

to travel by car
voyager en voiture
vwa-ya-ZHAY uh vwa-TEWR

to travel by bicycle
voyager en vélo
vwa-ya-ZHAY uh vay-LOH

to travel by motorcycle
voyager en voiture
vwa-ya-ZHAY uh mo-TOH

travel agency
l'agence de voyages
la-GOUNS duh-vwa-YAZH

family holiday
les vacances en famille
lay-va-KOUNS eh-fa-MEEY

safari
le safari
luh-sa-fa-REE

beach holiday
les vacances à la mer
lay-va-KOUNS a-la-MAYR

honeymoon
le voyage de noces
luh-vwa-YAZH duh-NOS

round-the-world trip
le voyage autour du monde
luh-vwa-YAZH oh-toor dew-MOHD

cruise
la croisière
la-krwa-ZYAYR

to book
réserver
ray-sehr-VAY

long-haul destination
la destination lointaine
la-dehs-tee-na-SYOH leh-TAYN

guided tour
la visite guidée
la-vee-SSET gee-DAY

out of season
hors saison
ohr say-SOH

picturesque village
le village pittoresque
luh-vee-LAZH pee-toh-RAYSK

landscape
le paysage
luh-payy-ZAZH

to go sightseeing
visiter
vee-zee-TAY

city break
le séjour en ville
luh-say-ZHOOR eh-VEEL

holiday brochure	**la brochure de vacances**	la-bro-SHEWR duh-va-KOUNS
holiday destination	**la destination de vacances**	la-days-tee-na-SYON duh-va-KOUNS
package tour	**le voyage organisé**	luh-vwa-YAZH or-ga-nee-ZAY
places of interest	**les lieux d'intérêt**	lay-LYEH deh-tay-RAY
short break	**le court séjour**	luh-KOOR say-ZHOOR
tourist attractions	**les attractions touristiques**	lay-za-tra-XYON too-rees-TEEK
tourist trap	**le piège à touristes**	luh-PYAYZH a-too-REEST

Afghanistan
l'Afghanistan
laf-ga-nees-TOUN

Albania
l'Albanie
lal-ba-NEE

Algeria
l'Algérie
lal-zhay-REE

Andorra
l'Andorre
loun-DOR

Angola
l'Angola
loun-go-LAH

Antigua and Barbuda
Antigua-et-Barbuda
oun-tee-GA-ay-bar-bew-DAH

Argentina
l'Argentine
lar-zhoun-TEEN

Armenia
l'Arménie
lar-may-NEE

Aruba
Aruba
a-rew-BA

Australia
l'Australie
lohs-tra-LEE

Austria
l'Autriche
loh-TREESH

Azerbaijan
l'Azerbaïdjan
la-zayr-bai-ZHOUN

The Bahamas
les Bahamas
lay-ba-ah-MAH

Bahrain
Bahreïn
bah-RAIN

Bangladesh
le Bangladesh
lyh-boun-gla-DAYSH

Barbados
la Barbade
la-bar-BAD

Belarus
la Biélorussie
la-byay-lo-rew-SEE

Belgium
la Belgique
la-bayl-ZHEEK

Belize
le Belize
lyh-beh-LEEZ

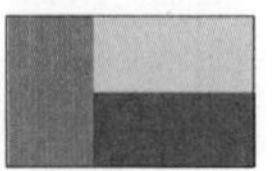
Benin
le Bénin
lyh-bay-NEH

Bhutan
le Bhoutan
lyh-boo-TOUN

Brazil
le Brésil
lyh-bray-ZEEL

Burma
la Birmanie
la-beer-ma-NEE

Canada
le Canada
lyh-ka-na-DAH

Chile
le Chili
lyh-tchee-LEE

Bolivia
la Bolivie
la-bo-lee-VEE

Brunei
le Brunei
lyh-brew-NEE

Burundi
le Burundi
lyh-bew-rewn-DEE

Cape Verde
le Cap-Vert
lyh-kap-VAYR

China
la Chine
la-SHEEN

Bosnia and Herzegovina
la Bosnie-Herzégovine
la-bos-NEE-ayr-zay-go-VEEN

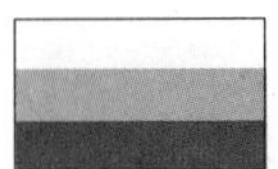

Bulgaria
la Bulgarie
la-bewl-ga-REE

Cambodia
le Cambodge
lyh-kah-BOZH

Central African Republic
la République centrafricaine
la-ray-pew-BLEEK sawntr-a-free-KAYN

Colombia
la Colombie
la-ko-loh-BEE

Botswana
le Botswana
lyh-bos-va-NAH

Burkina Faso
le Burkina Faso
lyh-bewr-kee-NA fa-SOH

Cameroon
le Cameroun
lyh-ka-may-ROON

Chad
le Tchad
luh-TCHAD

Comoros
les Comores
lay-ko-MOR

Democratic Republic of the Congo
la République Démocratique du Congo
la-ray-pew-BLEEK day-mo-kra-TEEK dew-Koh-GOH

Republic of the Congo
la République du Congo
la-ray-pew-BLEEK dew-koh-GOH

Costa Rica
le Costa Rica
lyh-kos-TA ree-KA

Côte d'Ivoire
la Côte d'Ivoire
la-KOT dee-VWAR

Croatia
la Croatie
la-kro-a-SEE

Cuba
Cuba
kew-BA

Curacao
le Curaçao
lyh-kew-ra-sa-OH

Cyprus
Chypre
sheepr

Czechia
la République tchèque
la-ray-pew-BLEEK TCHAYK

Denmark
le Danemark
lyh-dayn-MARK

Djibouti
Djibouti
zhee-boo-TEE

Dominica
la Dominique
la-do-mee-NEEK

Dominican Republic
la République Dominicaine
la-ray-pew-BLEEK domee-nee-KAYN

East Timor
le Timor oriental
lyh-tee-MOR oh-rieh-TAL

Ecuador
l'Équateur
laykwa-TEHR

Egypt
l'Egypte
lay-ZHEEPT

El Salvador
le Salvador
lyh-sal-va-DOR

Equatorial Guinea
la Guinée Équatoriale
la-gee-NAY ay-kwa-to-RYAL

Eritrea
l'Érythrée
lay-ree-TRAY

Estonia
l'Estonie
lehs-to-NEE

France
la France
la-FROUNS

Germany
l'Allemagne
la-lay-MANY

Guatemala
le Guatemala
luh-gwa-teh-ma-LAH

Haiti
Haïti
ha-ee-TEE

Ethiopia
l'Ethiopie
leh-tyo-PEE

Gabon
le Gabon
lyh-ga-BOH

Ghana
le Ghana
lyh-ga-NA

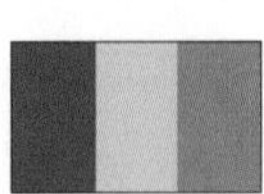

Guinea
la Guinée
la-gee-NAY

Honduras
le Honduras
lyh-hoh-dew-RA

Fiji
les îles Fidji
lay-ZEEL fee-ZHEE

The Gambia
la Gambie
la-gah-BEE

Greece
la Grèce
la-GRAYS

Guinea-Bissau
la Guinée-Bissau
la-gee-NAY-bee-SOH

Hong Kong
Hong Kong
hoh-KOH

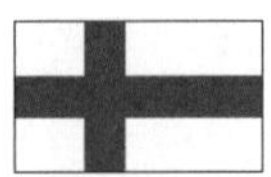

Finland
la Finlande
la-feh-LOUND

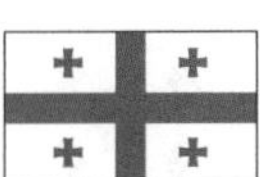

Georgia
la Géorgie
la-zhay-or-ZHEE

Grenada
la Grenade
la-greh-NAD

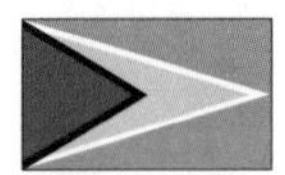

Guyana
la Guyane
la-gew-YAN

Hungary
la Hongrie
la-oh-GREE

Iceland
l'Islande
lees-LOUND

India
l'Inde
LEHD

Indonesia
l'Indonésie
leh-do-nay-SEE

Iran
l'Iran
lee-ROUN

Iraq
l'Irak
lee-RAK

Ireland
l'Irlande
leer-LOUND

Israel
Israël
ee-zra-AYL

Italy
l'Italie
lee-ta-LEE

Jamaica
la Jamaïque
la-zha-MAIK

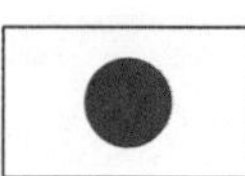
Japan
le Japon
lyh-zha-POH

Jordan
la Jordanie
la-zhor-da-NEE

Kazakhstan
le Kazakhstan
lyh-ka-zakh-stoun

Kenya
le Kenya
lyh-keh-NYA

Kiribati
Kiribati
kee-ree-ba-TEE

North Korea
la Corée du Nord
la-ko-RAY dew-NOR

South Korea
la Corée du Sud
la-koh-RAY dew-SEWD

Kosovo
le Kosovo
lyh-ko-so-VOH

Kuwait
le Koweït
lyh-ko-WEIT

Kyrgyzstan
le Kirghizistan
lyh-keer-geez-zee-STOUN

Laos
le Laos
lyh-la-OS

Latvia
la Lettonie
la-leh-to-NEE

Lebanon
le Liban
lyh-lee-BOUN

Lesotho
le Lesotho
lyh-leh-so-TOH

Liberia
le Libéria
lyh-lee-bay-RYA

Libya
la Libye
la-lee-BEE

Liechtenstein
le Liechtenstein
lyh-leesh-ten-STEIN

Lithuania
la Lituanie
la-lee-tew-a-NEE

Luxembourg
le Luxembourg
lyh-lew-xeh-BOORG

Macau
Macao
ma-ka-OH

Macedonia
la Macédoine
la-ma-say-DWAN

Madagascar
Madagascar
ma-da-gas-KAR

Malawi
le Malawi
lyh-ma-la-WEE

Malaysia
la Malaisie
la-ma-lay-SEE

Maldives
les Maldives
lay-ma-la-DEEV

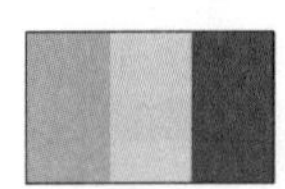
Mali
le Mali
lyh-ma-LEE

Malta
Malte
malt

Marshall Islands
les îles Marshall
lay-ZEEL mar-SHAL

Mauritania
la Mauritanie
la-mo-ree-ta-NEE

Mauritius
Maurice
mo-REES

Mexico
le Mexique
lyh-may-XEEK

Micronesia
la Micronésie
la-mee-kro-nay-SEE

Montenegro
le Monténégro
luh-moh-tay-nay-GROH

Nauru
Nauru
noh-REW

Nicaragua
le Nicaragua
lyh-nee-ka-ra-gew-AH

Oman
Oman
oh-MAN

Moldova
la Moldavie
la-molda-VEE

Morocco
le Maroc
luh-ma-ROK

Nepal
le Népal
lyh-nay-PAL

Niger
le Niger
lyh-nee-ZHAYR

Pakistan
le Pakistan
lyh-pa-kees-TOUN

Monaco
Monaco
mo-na-KOH

Mozambique
le Mozambique
lyh-mo-zah-BEEK

Netherlands
les Pays-Bas
lay-pay-EE-ba

Nigeria
le Nigeria
lyh-nee-zhay-RYA

Palau
les Palaos
lay-pa-la-OH

Mongolia
la Mongolie
la-moh-go-LEE

Namibia
la Namibie
ma-na-mee-BEE

New Zealand
la Nouvelle-Zélande
la-noo-VEL-zay-LOUND

Norway
la Norvège
la-nor-VAYZH

Palestinian Territories
les Territoires palestiniens
lay-teh-ree-TWAR pa-lays-tee-NAWN

Panama
le Panama
lyh-pa-na-MA

Papua New Guinea
la Papouasie-Nouvelle-Guinée
la-pa-poo-a-SEE-noo-VAYL-gee-NAY

Paraguay
le Paraguay
lyh-pa-ra-GWAY

Peru
le Pérou
lyh-pay-ROO

Philippines
les Philippines
lay-fee-lee-PEEN

Poland
la Pologne
la-po-LONY

Portugal
le Portugal
lyh-por-tew-GAL

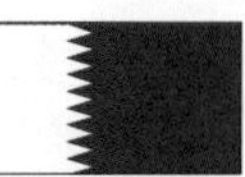

Qatar
le Qatar
leh-ka-TAR

Romania
la Roumanie
la-roo-ma-NEE

Russia
la Russie
la-rew-SEE

Rwanda
le Rwanda
lyh-rwoun-DA

Saint Lucia
Sainte-Lucie
seh-lew-SEE

Samoa
Samoa
sa-moh-AH

San Marino
Saint-Marin
seh0mar-TEH

Saudi Arabia
l'Arabie Saoudite
la-ra-BEE sow-DEET

Senegal
le Sénégal
lyh-sya-nay-GAL

Serbia
la Serbie
la-sehr-BEE

Seychelles
les Seychelles
lay-zay-SHAYL

Sierra Leone
la Sierra Leone
la-syayr-RA lay-oh-NAY

Singapore
Singapour
seh-ga-POOR

Sint Maarten
Saint Martin
seh-mar-TEH

Slovakia
la Slovaquie
la-slo-va-KEE

Slovenia
la Slovénie
la-slo-VAY-NEE

Solomon Islands
les îles Salomon
lay-ZEEL sa-lo-MOH

Somalia
la Somalie
la-so-ma-LEE

South Africa
l'Afrique du Sud
la-FREEK dew-SEWD

Spain
l'Espagne
lays-PANY

Sri Lanka
le Sri Lanka
lyh-sree-lan-KAH

Sudan
le Soudan
lyh-soo-DOUN

South Sudan
le Soudan du sud
lyh-soo-DOUN dew-SEWD

Suriname
le Surinam
lyh-sew-ree-NAM

Swaziland
le Swaziland
lyh-swoh-zee-LOUND

Sweden
la Suède
la-swee-AYD

Switzerland
la Suisse
la-SWEES

Syria
la Syrie
la-see-REE

Taiwan
Taïwan
tie-WAN

Tajikistan
le Tadjikistan
lyh-ta-zhee-kees-TOUN

Tanzania
la Tanzanie
la-tan-za-NEE

Thailand
la Thaïlande
la-tie-LOUD

Togo
le Togo
lyh-to-GOH

Turkey
la Turquie
la-tewr-KEE

Ukraine
l'Ukraine
lew-KRAIN

Uruguay
l'Uruguay
lew-rew-GAY

Vietnam
le Vietnam
lyh-vyayt-NAM

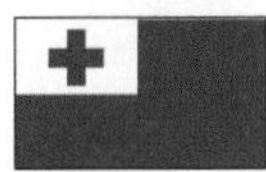
Tonga
les Tonga
lay-toh-GAH

Turkmenistan
le Turkménistan
lyh-tewrk-may-nees-TOUN

United Arab Emirates
les Emirats arabes unis
lay-zay-mee-RA a-RAB ew-NEE

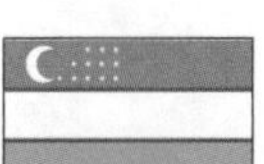
Uzbekistan
l'Ouzbékistan
looz-bay-kees-TOUN

Yemen
le Yémen
luh-yay-MAYN

Trinidad and Tobago
Trinité-et-Tobago
tree-nee-TAY-ay-toh-bah-GOH

Tuvalu
Tuvalu
tew-vah-LEW

United Kingdom
le Royaume-Uni
lyh-rwa-YOM ew-NEE

Vanuatu
Vanuatu
vah-nyah-TEW

Zambia
la Zambie
la-zah-BEE

Tunisia
la Tunisie
la-tew-nee-SEE

Uganda
l'Ouganda
loo-goun-DAH

United States of America
les Etats-Unis d'Amérique
lay-zay-TA-zew-NEE da-may-REEK

Venezuela
le Venezuela
lyh-veh-neh-zoo-ay-LA

Zimbabwe
le Zimbabwe
luh-zeem-bab-WAY

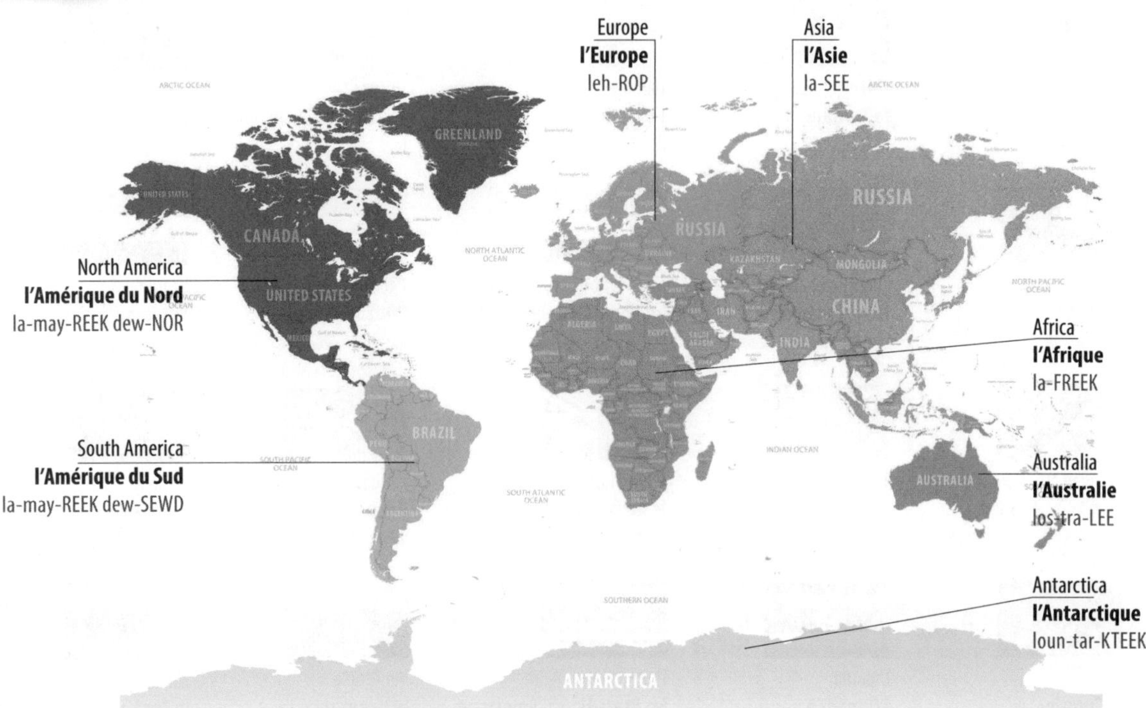
Europe
l'Europe
leh-ROP
Asia
l'Asie
la-SEE
North America
l'Amérique du Nord
la-may-REEK dew-NOR
Africa
l'Afrique
la-FREEK
South America
l'Amérique du Sud
la-may-REEK dew-SEWD
Australia
l'Australie
los-tra-LEE
Antarctica
l'Antarctique
loun-tar-KTEEK
ARCTIC OCEAN
GREENLAND
CANADA
UNITED STATES
RUSSIA
KAZAKHSTAN
MONGOLIA
CHINA
IRAN
INDIA
NORTH ATLANTIC OCEAN
NORTH PACIFIC OCEAN
BRAZIL
SOUTH PACIFIC OCEAN
SOUTH ATLANTIC OCEAN
INDIAN OCEAN
AUSTRALIA
SOUTHERN OCEAN
ANTARCTICA

bus stop
l'arrêt de bus
la-RAY duh-BEWS

platform
le quai
luh-KAY

(aero)plane
l'avion
la-VYOH

moped / scooter
le scooter
luh-skoo-TEHR

(bi)cycle
le vélo
luh-vay-LOH

boat
le bateau
luh-bah-TOH

bus
le bus
luh-BEWS

ship
le navire
luh-na-VEER

car
la voiture
la-vwa-TEWR

helicopter
l'hélicoptère
lay-lee-ko-PTAYR

lorry
le camion
luh-ka-MYOH

tanker
le pétrolier
luh-pay-troh-LYAY

kid's scooter
la trotinette
la-troh-tee-NAYT

(motor)bike
la moto
la-moh-TOH

train
le train
luh-TREH

taxi
le taxi
luh-ta-XEE

ferry
le ferry
luh-feh-REE

submarine
le sous-marin
luh-soo-ma-REH

sailing boat
le voiler
luh-YOT

tram
le tram
luh-TRAM

by air	**par avion**	par-a-VYOH	in the port	**dans le port**	doun luh-POR
on the motorway	**sur l'autoroute**	sewr loh-toh-ROOT	by rail	**par chemin de fer**	par sheh-MEH duh-FAYR
on the road	**sur la route**	sewr la-ROOT	by tube / underground	**en métro**	eh-may-TROH
by sea	**par voie maritime**	par vwa ma-ree-TEEM	on foot	**à pied**	a-PYAY

airport
l'aéroport
la-ay-roh-POR

arrivals
les arrivées
lay-zah-ree-VAY

departures
les départs
lay-day-PAR

luggage
les bagages
lay-ba-GAZH

carry-on luggage
les bagages à main
lay-ba-GAZH a-MEH

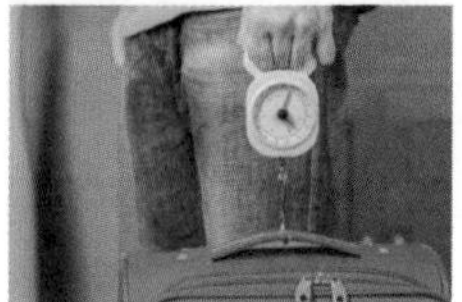

oversized baggage
l'excédent de bagages
leh-xay-DAWN duh-ba-GAZH

check-in desk
le comptoir d'enregistrement
luh-koh-TWAR deh-reh-zhees-tray-MOUN

customs
la douane
la-DOOAN

baggage reclaim
la zone de retrait des bagages
la-ZON duh-reh-TRAY day-ba-GAZH

boarding pass
la carte d'embarquement
la-KART deh-bar-kay-MOUN

flight ticket
le billet
luh-bee-YAY

economy class
la classe économique
la-KLAS ay-koh-noh-MEEK

business class
la classe affaires
la-KLAS a-FAYR

arrivals lounge
le hall d'arrivée
luh-OHL-da-ree-VAY

delayed
retardé
reh-tar-DAY

to board a plane
embarquer dans un avion
eh-bar-KAY doun-zeh-na-VYOH

gate
la porte
la-PORT

passport
le passeport
lyh-pas-POR

passport control
le contrôle des passeports
luh-koh-TROL day-pas-POR

security check
le contrôle de sécurité
luh-koh-TROL duh-say-kew-ree-TAY

airline	**la compagnie aérienne**	la-koh-pah-NEE a-ay-RYAYN
boarding time	**l'heure d'embarquement**	lehr deh-bar-kay-MOUN
charter flight	**le vol charter**	luh-VOL shar-TAYR
long-haul flight	**le vol long-courrier**	luh-VOL loh-koo-RYAY
on time	**à temps**	a-TEH
one-way ticket	**l'aller simple**	la-LAY sehpl

return ticket	**le billet aller-retour**	luh-bee-YAY a-LAY-reh-TOOR
The flight has been delayed.	**Le vol a été retardé.**	luh-VOL a-ay-TAY reh-tar-DAY
to book a ticket to	**acheter un billet pour**	ash-TAY eh-bee-YAY poor

railway station
la gare
la-GAR

train
le train
luh-TREH

platform
le quai
luh-KAY

express train	**le train express**	luh-TREH ayx-PRAYS
to get on the train	**prendre le train**	prawndr luh-TREH
to get off the train	**descendre du train**	duh-SEHDR dew treh
to miss a train	**rater le train**	ra-TAY luh-TREH

train driver
le conducteur
luh-koh-dewk-TEHR

travelcard
le titre de transport
luh-TEETR duh-trans-POR

carriage
la voiture
la-vwa-TEWR

seat
le siège
luh-SYAYZH

train journey
le trajet en train
luh-tra-ZHAY awn-TREH

station
la gare
la-GAR

restaurant car
le wagon-restaurant
luh-va-GOH-rehs-toh-ROUN

sleeper train
le train couchette
luh-TREH koo-SHAYT

toilet
les toilettes
lay-twa-LAYT

coach
le car
luh-KAR

bus driver
le chauffeur de bus
luh-shoh-FEHR duh-BEWS

bus stop
l'arrêt de bus
la-RAY duh-BEWS

validator
le composteur de billets
luh-koh-post-EHR duh-bee-YAY

double-decker bus
le bus à deux étages
luh-BEWS a-deh-zay-TAZH

bus journey
le trajet de bus
luh-tra-ZHAY duh-BEWS

coach station
la gare routière
la-GAR roo-TYAYR

request stop
l'arrêt sur demande
la-ray sewr duh-MOUND

bus fare	**le ticket de bus**	luh-tee-KAY duh-BEWS
the next stop	**le prochain arrêt**	luh-proh-SHEH a-RAY
night bus	**le bus de nuit**	luh-BEWS duh-NWEE
to get on the bus	**prendre le bus**	prehdr luh-BEWS
to get off the bus	**descendre du bus**	duh-SAWNDR dew bews
to miss a bus	**rater le bus**	ra-TAY luh-BEWS

hotel
l'hôtel
loh-TAYL

campsite
le terrain de camping
luh-tayr-EH duh-kawn-PEENG

holiday resort
le lieu de villégiature
luh-LYEH duh-vee-lay-zhya-TUR

youth hostel
l'auberge de jeunesse
loh-BAYRZG duh-zheh-NAYS

all-inclusive	**tout compris**	too koh-PREE
self-catering	**repas non compris**	reh-PAH noh-koh-PREE
full-board	**la pension complète**	la-pawn-SYOH koh-PLAYT
half-board	**la demi-pension**	la-duh-MEE-peh-SYOH
accommodation	**l'hébergement**	lay-bayr-zhay-MAWN
I'm looking for a place to stay.	**Je cherche un hébergement.**	zhuh shayrsh eh ay-behr-zhay-MAWN.
Can you recommend a hotel?	**Pouvez-vous me recommander un hôtel ?**	poo-vay-VOO meh reh-koh-moun-DAY eh-noh-tAYL ?
We are staying at the hotel "XZ".	**Nous sommes descendus à l'hôtel "XZ".**	noo-SOM duh-sawn-DEW a-loh-TAYL „XY".
Have you already booked the hotel?	**Avez-vous déjà réservé la chambre à l'hôtel ?**	a-vay-VOO day-ZHAH ray-sehr-VAY la-SHOUNBR a-loh-TAYL ?

bed and breakfast
la chambre d'hôte
la-SHOUNBR DOHT

single bed
le lit simple
luh-LEE sehpl

double bed
le lit double
luh-LEE doobl

floor
l'étage
lay-TAZH

front desk / reception
la réception
la-ray-seh-PSYOH

hotel manager
le directeur de l'hôtel
luh-dee-rayk-TEHR duh-loh-TAYL

indoor pool
la piscine intérieure
la-pee-SEEN eh-tay-RYEHR

key
la clé
la-KLAY

kitchenette
le coin cuisine
luh-KWEH kwee-ZEEN

luggage cart
le chariot à bagages
luh-shah-RYOH a-ba-GAZH

towels
les serviettes
lay-sehr-VYAYT

room service
le service de chambre
luh-sehr-VEES duh-SHAHBR

lobby
le hall d'entrée
luh-OHL dawn-TRAY

wake-up call
le réveil par téléphone
luh-ray-VEY par tay-lay-FON

reservation
la réservation
la-ray-sehr-va-SYOH

guest
le client
luh-klee-EH

check-in	**l'arrivée**	la-ree-VAY
check-out	**le départ**	luh-day-PAR
complimentary breakfast	**petit-déjeuner inclus**	peh-tee-day-zheh-NAY eh-KLEW
queen-size bed	**le grand lit**	luh-GROUN lee
king-size bed	**le très grand lit**	luh treh-GROUN lee
late charge	**le supplément de retard**	luh-sew-play-MAWN duh-reh-TAR
full	**complet**	koh-PLAY
parking pass	**le permis de stationnement**	luh-payr-MEE duh-stah-syoh-nay-MAWN
pay-per-view movie	**le film à la carte**	luh-FEELM a-la-KART
rate	**le prix**	luh-PREE
vacancy	**la disponibilité**	la-dees-pohonee-bee-le-TAY

city-centre / downtown
le centre-ville
luh-sehtr-VEEL

capital
la capitale
la-kah-pee-TAL

centre
le centre
luh-SAWNTR

district
le quartier
luh-kar-TYAY

industrial zone
la zone industrielle
la-ZON eh-dew-STRYAYL

city
la ville
la-VEEL

metropolis
la métropole
la-may-troh-POL

region
la région
la-ray-ZGYOH

seaside resort
la station balnéaire
la-sta-TION bal-nay-AYR

old town
la vieille ville
la-vyayy-VEEL

ski resort
la station de ski
la-sta-SYOH duh-SKEE

small town
la commune
la-ko-MEWN

suburb
la banlieue
la-boun-LYEH

village
le village
luh-vee-LAZG

winter resort
la station de sports d'hiver
la-sta-SYOH duh-SPOR dee-VAYR

alley
l'allée
la-LAY

boulevard
le boulevard
luh-bool-VAR

motorway
l'autoroute
loh-toh-ROOT

toll road
la route à péage
la-ROOT a pay-AZH

country road
la route de campagne
la-ROOT duh-kah-PANY

street
la rue
la-REW

bicycle lane
la voie cyclable
la-VWA see-KLABL

bicycle path
la piste cyclable
la-PEEST see-KLABL

crossroads / intersection
le carrefour
luh-kar-FOOR

traffic lights
les feux de circulation
luh-FEH duh-seer-kew-la-SYOH

red light
le feu rouge
luh-FEH ROOZH

orange light
le feu orange
luh-FEH oh-ROUNZH

green light
le feu vert
luh-FEH vehr

roundabout
le rond-point
luh-roh-PWEH

pedestrian crossing
le passage piétons
luh-pa-SAZH pyay-TOH

pavement
le trottoir
luh-troh-TWAR

bridge
le pont
luh-POH

footbridge
la passerelle
la pas-RAYL

overpass
La route surélevée
la-ROOT sewr-ay-lay-VAY

underpass
le passage souterrain
luh-pa-SAZH soo-teh-REH

tunnel
le tunnel
luh-tew-NAYL

road
la route
la-ROOT

street corner
le coin de la rue
luh-KWEH duh-la-REW

one-way street
la rue à sens unique
la-REW a-SEHS ew-NEEK

avenue	**l'avenue**	la-veh-NEW
two-lane road	**la route à double voie**	la-ROOT a-DOOBL vwa
four-lane road	**la route à quatre voies**	la-ROOT a-katr-VWA
main road	**la rue principale**	la-REW preh-see-PAL
side street	**la rue transversale**	la-REW trouns-vayr-SAL
expressway	**la voie express**	la-VWA ayx-PRAYS
fast lane	**la voie rapide**	la-VWA ra-PEED
left lane	**la voie de gauche**	la-VWA duh-GOSH
right lane	**la voie de droite**	la-VWA duh-DRWAT
breakdown lane	**la bande d'arrêt d'urgence**	la-BOUND da-RAY dewr-ZHAWNS

attractions
les sites touristiques
lay-SEET too-rees-TEEK

casino
le casino
luh-kah-see-NOH

guide book
le guide de voyage
luh-GEED duh-vwa-YAZH

park
le parc
luh-PARK

guided tour
la visite guidée
la-vee-ZEET gee-DAY

information
l'information touristique
leh-for-ma-SYOH too-rees-TEEK

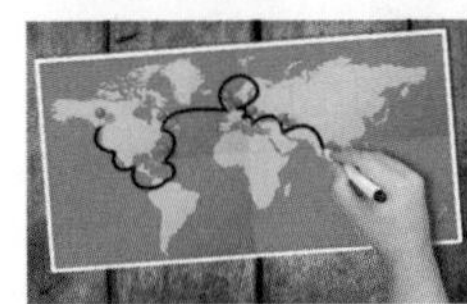

itinerary
l'itinéraire
lee-tee-nay-RAYR

ruins
les ruines
lay-rew-EEN

monument
le monument
luh-moh-new-MAWN

museum
le musée
luh-mew-ZAY

national park
le parc national
luh-PARK na-syoh-NAL

sightseeing
la visite
la-vee-ZEET

souvenirs
les souvenirs
lay-soo-vay-NEER

tour bus
le bus touristique
luh-BEWS too-rees-TEEK

tourist
le/la touriste
luh/la too-REEST

entrance fee / price	**le prix d'entrée**	luh-PREE dawn-TRAY
to buy a souvenir	**acheter un souvenir**	ash-TAY eh-soo-vay-NEER
to do a tour	**la visite guidée**	la-vee-ZEET gee-DAY
tour guide	**le guide**	luh-GEED

airport
l'aéroport
la-ay-roh-POR

bank
la banque
la-BOUNK

bus stop
l'arrêt de bus
la-RAY duh-BEWS

church
l'église
lay-GLEEZ

cinema
le cinéma
luh-see-nay-MA

city / town hall
la mairie / l'hôtel de ville
la-may-REE / loh-TAYL duh-VEEL

department store
le centre commercial
luh-SAWNTR ko-mayr-SYAL

factory
l'usine
lew-ZEEN

fire station
la caserne de pompiers
la-ka-ZAYRN de-poh-PYAY

hospital
l'hôpital
loh-pee-TAL

hotel
l'hôtel
loh-TAYL

library
la bibliothèque
la-bee-blyoh-TAYK

theatre
le théâtre
luh-tay-ATR

museum
le musée
luh-mew-ZAY

parking area
le parking
luh-par-KEENG

playground
l'aire de jeu
layr-duh-ZHEH

police station
le commissariat de police
luh-koh-mee-sa-RYA duh-poh-LEES

post office
le bureau de poste
luh-bew-ROH duh-POST

prison
la prison
la-pree-SOH

restaurant
le restaurant
luh-rehs-toh-ROUN

school
l'école
lay-KOL

taxi stand
la station de taxis
la-stah-SYOH duh-ta-XEE

harbour
le port
luh-POR

square
la place
la-PLAS

supermarket
le supermarché
luh-sew-payr-mar-SHAY

railway station
la gare
la-GAR

How do I get to the railway station?	**Comment se rend-on à la gare ?**	koh-mawn seh-rawn-doh a-la-GAR ?
Where can I find a taxi?	**Où puis-je trouver un taxi ?**	OO pweezh troo-VAY eh-ta-XEE ?

mask
le masque
luh-MASK

snorkel
le tuba
luh-tew-BA

swimming goggles
les lunettes de natation
lay-lew-NAYT duh-na-ta-SYOH

beach ball
le ballon de plage
luh-bah-LOH duh-PLAZH

hat
le chapeau
luh-shah-POH

sunglasses
les lunettes de soleil
lay-lew-NAYT duh-soh-LAYY

sunscreen
la crème solaire
la-KRAYM soh-LAYR

beach towel
la serviette de plage
la-sehr-VYAYT duh-PLAZH

beach
la plage
la-PLAZH

sun lounger
la chaise longue
la-shayz-LOHG

swimming cap	**le bonnet de bain**	luh-boh-NAY duh-BEH
bikini	**le bikini**	luh-bee-kee-NEE
swimming costume	**le maillot de bain**	luh-ma-YOH duh-BEH
to sunbathe	**bronzer**	broh-ZAY
to swim	**nager**	nah-ZHAY

HEALTH

medicines
les médicaments
lay-may-dee-ka-MAWN

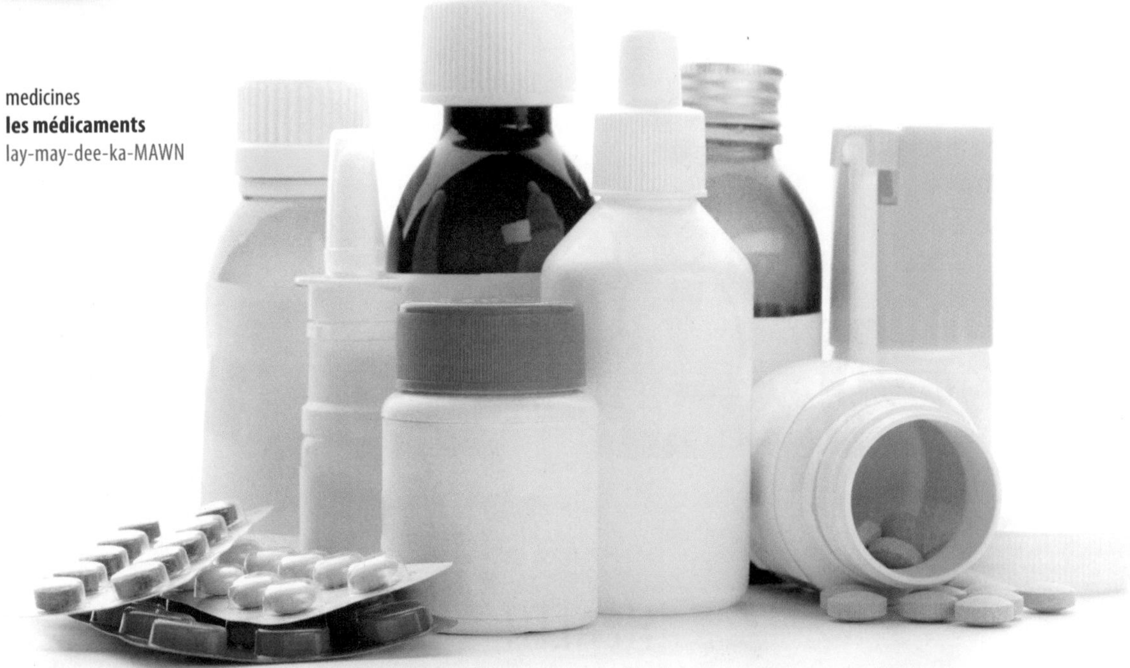

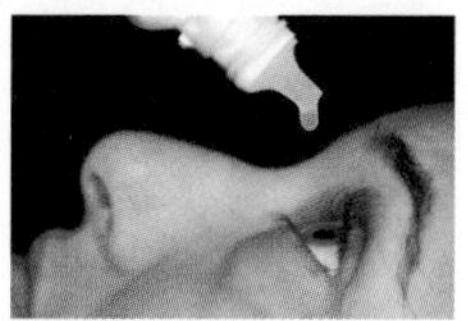
eye drops
les gouttes oculaires
lay-GOOT oh-kew-LAYR

painkiller
l'analgésique
la-nal-zhay-ZEEK

syrup
le sirop
luh-see-ROH

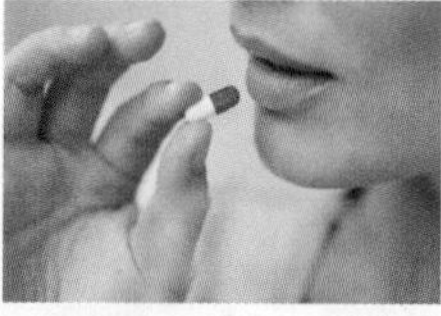
to take medicine
prendre des médicaments
prehdr day-may-dee-ka-MAWN

shot / injection
la vaccination
la-vak-see-na-SYOH

sleeping pill
le sédatif
luh-say-dah-TEEF

plaster
le pansement
luh-poun-seh-MAWN

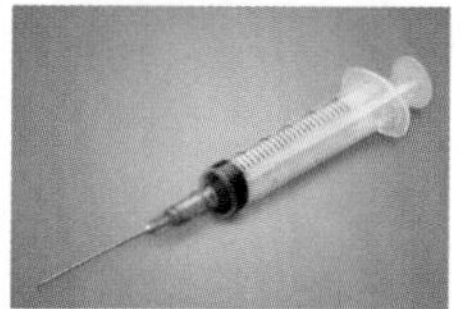
syringe
la seringue
luh-seh-REHG

gauze
la gaze
la-GAZ

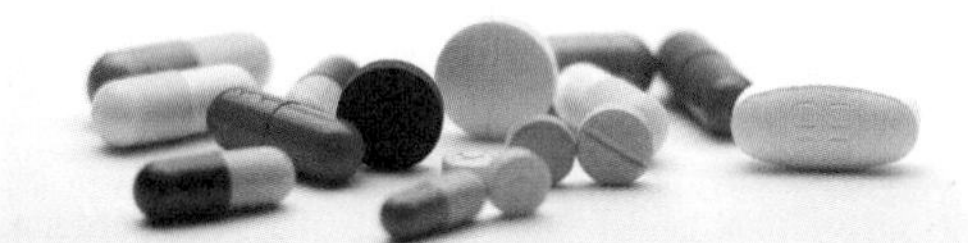
pill
la pilule
la-pee-LEWL

tablet
la gélule
la-ZHAY-LEWL

ointment
la pommade
la-poh-MAD

hospital
l'hôpital
loh-pee-TAL

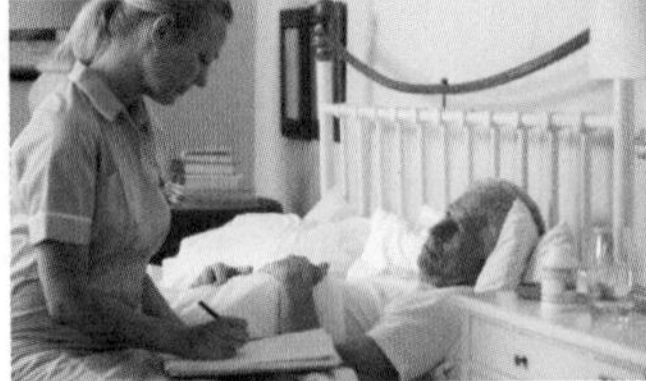

nurse
l'infirmier *m* / l'infirmière *f*
leh-fehr-MYAY / leh-fehr-MYAYR

doctor / physician
le / la médecin
luh/la mayd-SEH

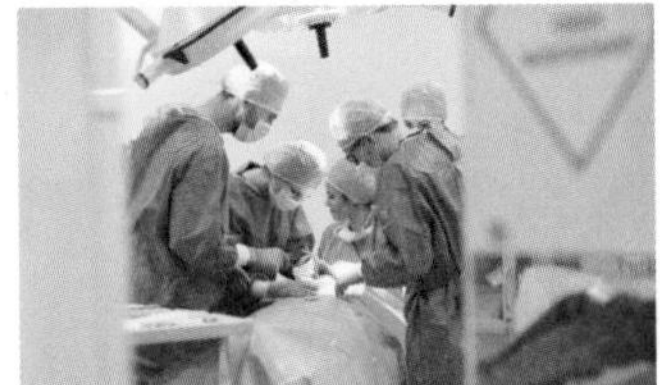

operation / surgery
l'opération
loh-pay-rah-SYOH

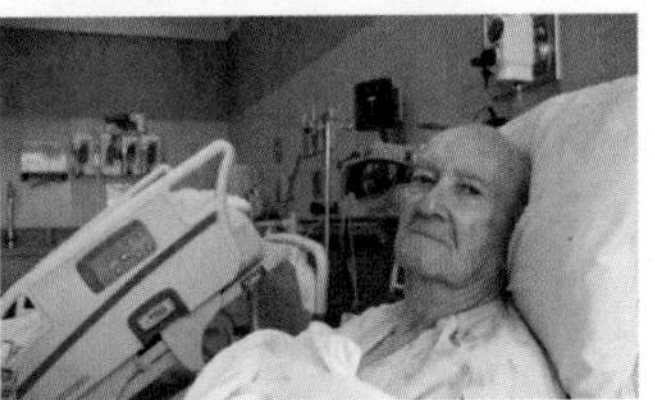

patient
le patient *m* / la patiente *f*
luh-pa-SYEH / la-pa-SYEH

waiting room
la salle d'attente
la-SAL da-TOUNT

check-up	**le bilan de santé**	luh-bee-LOUN duh-sah-TAY
diagnosis	**le diagnostic**	luh-dia-gnos-TEEK
pharmacy / chemist's	**la pharmacie**	la-far-ma-SEE

prescription	**l'ordonnance**	lor-doh-NOUNS
specialist	**le / la spécialiste**	luh / la-spay-sya-LEEST
treatment	**le traitement**	luh-trayt-MAWN

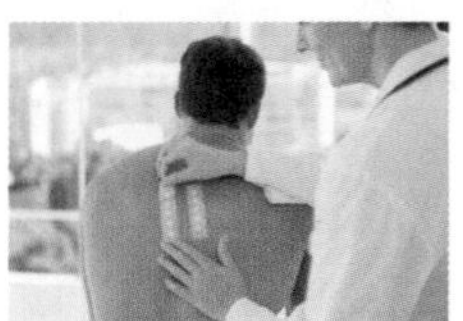

allergist
l'allergologue
la-lehr-goh-LOG

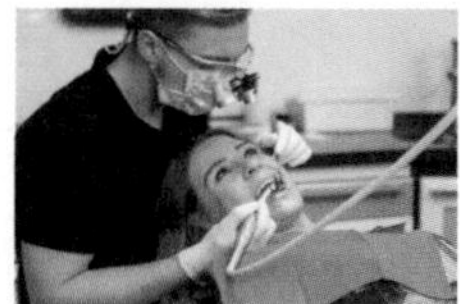

dentist
le / la dentiste
luh / la-dawn-TEEST

gynecologist
le / la gynécologue
luh / la-zhee-nay-koh-LOG

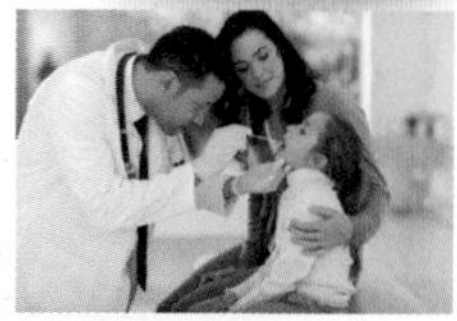

pediatrician
le / la pédiatre
luh / la-pay-DYATR

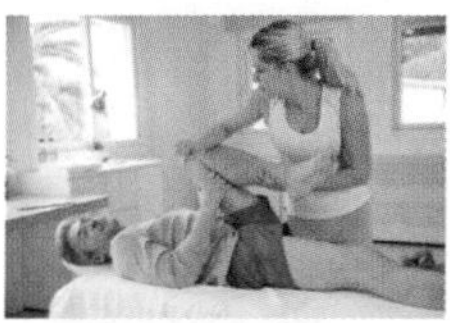

physiotherapist
le / la physiothérapeute
luh / la-fee-zyoh-tay-ra-PEHT

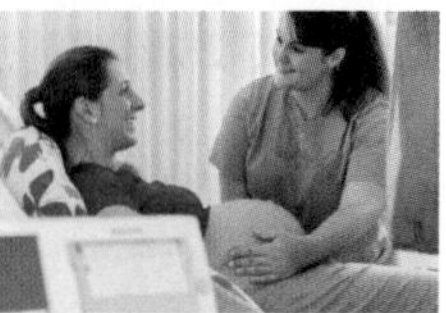

midwife
la sage-femme
la-SAZH fam

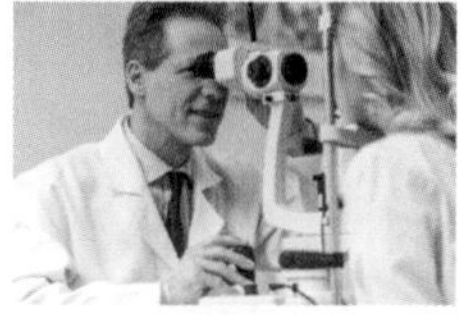

ophthalmologist
l'ophtalmologiste
lof-tal-mohploh-GEEST

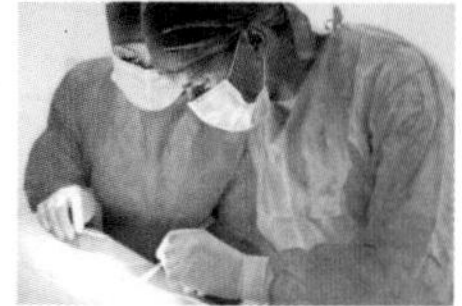

surgeon
le chirurgien *m* /
la chirurgienne *f*
luh-shee-roor-GYEH /
la-shee-roor-GYEHN

anaesthesiologist	**l'anesthésiste**	la-nays-tay-ZEEST
cardiologist	**le / la cardiologue**	luh / la-kar-dyoh-LOG
dermatologist	**le / la dermatologue**	luh / la-dehr-mah-toh-LOG
neurologist	**le / la neurologue**	luh / la-neh-roh-LOG
oncologist	**l'oncologue**	loh-koh-LOG
psychiatrist	**le / la psychiatre**	luh / la-psee-KYATR
radiologist	**le / la radiologue**	luh / la-ra-dyoh-LOG

to feel good
se sentir bien
seh-seh-TEER byeh

to catch a cold
attraper froid
a-tra-PAY frwa

to have a cold
avoir un rhume
a-VWAR eh-REWM

to sneeze
éternuer
ay-tayr-new-AY

to cough
tousser
too-SAY

to blow your nose
se moucher
seh-moo-SHAY

to feel sick
se sentir malade
seh-seh-TEER ma-LAD

to faint
s'évanouir
say-va-noo-EER

to pass out
perdre connaissance
payrdr ko-nay-SOUNS

to be tired
être fatigué *m* / fatiguée *f*
AYTR fa-tee-GAY

to be exhausted
être épuisé *m* / épuisée *f*
aytr ay-pwee-ZAY

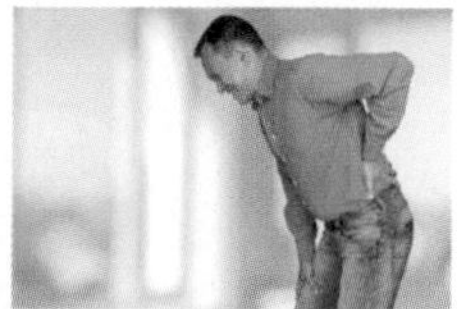
to have back pain
avoir mal au dos
a-VWAR mal-oh-DOH

to have earache
avoir mal aux oreilles
a-VWAR mal-oh-zoh-RAYY

to have a headache
avoir mal à la tête
a-VWAR mal-a-la-TAYT

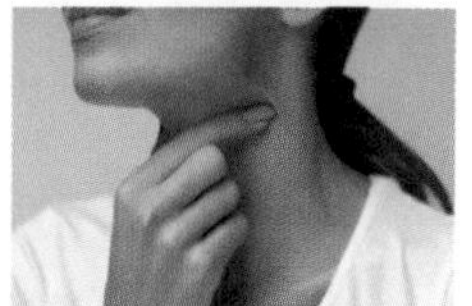
to have a sore throat
avoir mal à la gorge
a-VWAR mal-a-la-GORZH

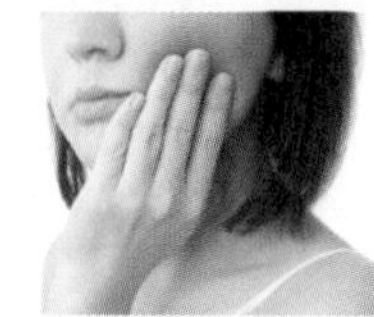
to have toothache
avoir mal aux dents
a-VWAR mal-oh-DEH

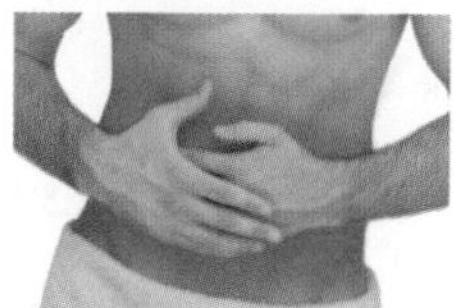
to have a stomach ache
avoir mal au ventre
a-VWAR mal-oh-VEHTR

to have a temperature
avoir de la fièvre
a-VWAR duh-la-FYEHVR

to have diarrhoea
avoir la diarrhée
a-VWAR la-dya-RAY

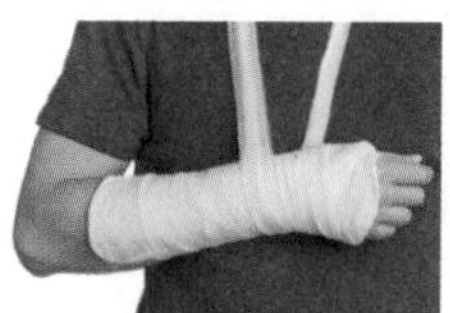
to break an arm
se casser le bras
seh-ka-SAY luh-BRA

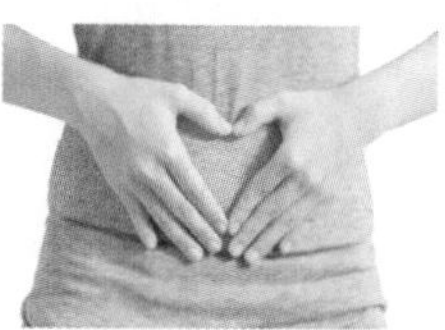
to be constipated
être constipé *m* / constipée *f*
aytr koh-stee-PAY

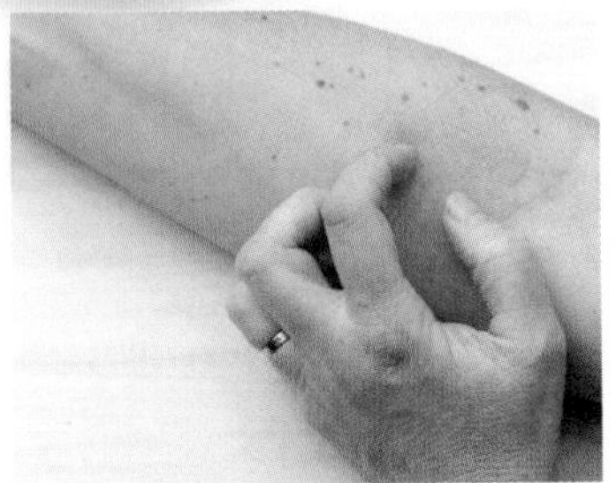

to have a rash
avoir une éruption cutanée
a-VWAR ewn-ay-rewp-SYOH kew-ta-NAY

to be allergic to
être allergique à
aytr a-layr-ZHEEK

to vomit
vomir
voh-MEER

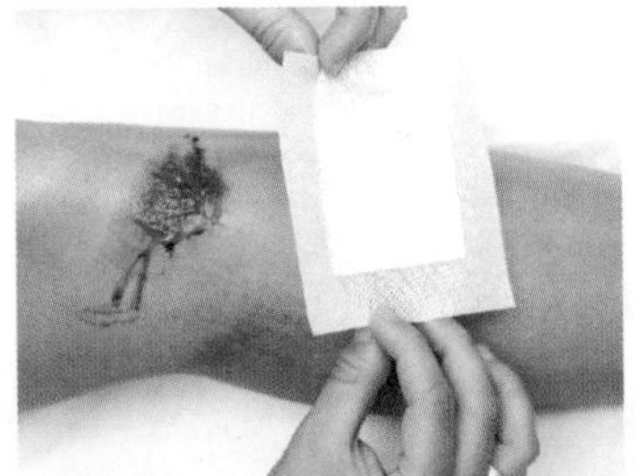

to hurt
avoir mal
a-VWAR mal

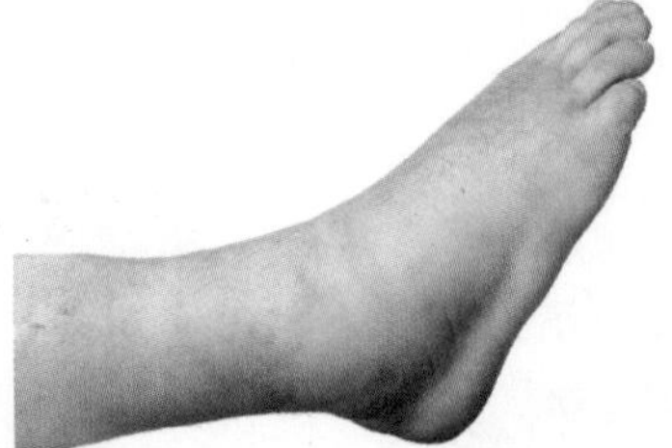

to swell
gonfler
goh-FLAY

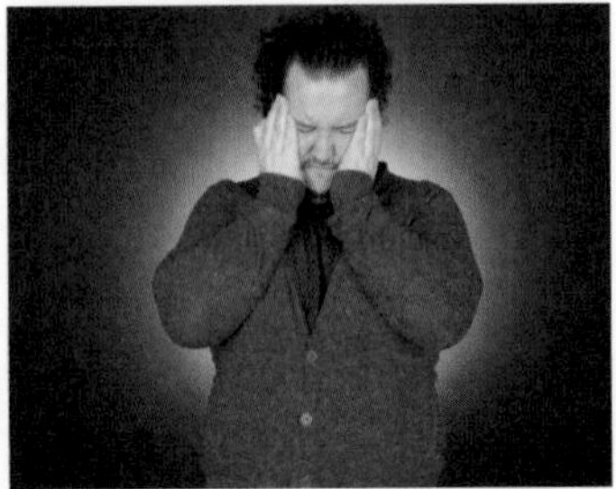

to suffer from
souffrir de
soo-FREER deh

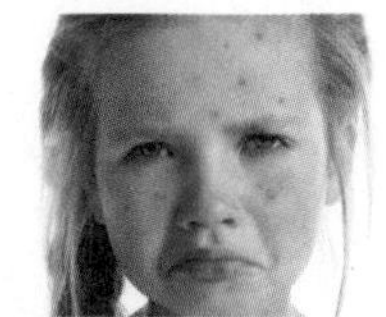

chicken pox
la varicelle
la-va-ree-SAYL

runny nose
le nez qui coule
luh-NAY kee-KOOL

cough
la toux
la-TOO

diarrhoea
la diarrhée
la-dia-RAY

heart attack
la crise cardiaque
la-KREEZ kar-DYAK

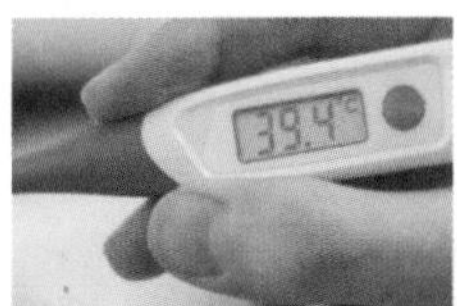

fever
la fièvre
la-FYEHVR

headache
le mal de tête
luh-MAL duh-TAYT

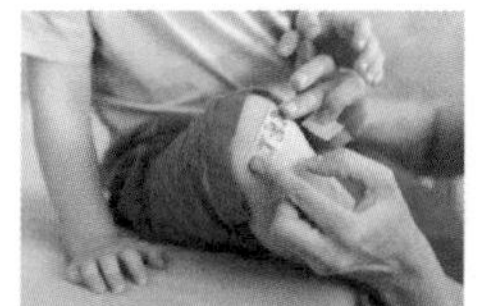

injury
la blessure
la-blay-SEWR

sore throat
le mal de gorge
luh-MAL duh-GORZH

asthma
l'asthme
lastm

flu
la grippe
la-GREEP

health
la santé
la-sah-TAY

hepatitis
l'hépatite
lay-pa-TEE

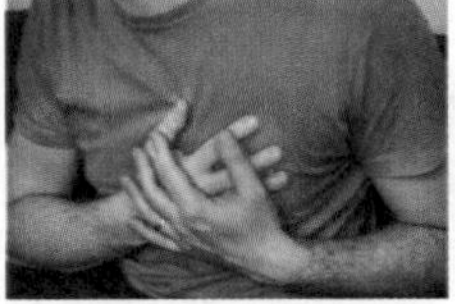
heart disease
la maladie cardio-vasculaire
la-ma-la-DEE kar-dio-vas-kew-LAYR

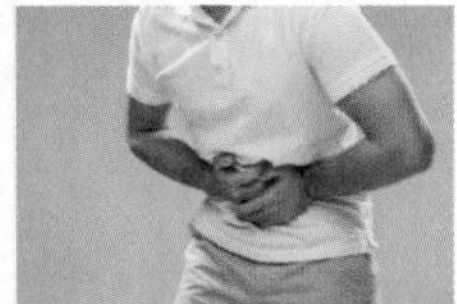
stomach ache
le mal de ventre
luh-MAL duh-VAWNTR

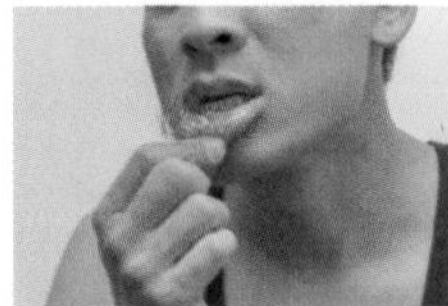
mouth ulcer
l'aphte
LAFT

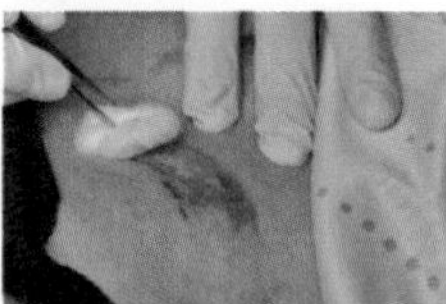
wound
la plaie
la-PLAY

common cold	**le rhume**	luh-REWM
fracture	**la fracture**	la-frak-TEWR
illness	**la maladie**	la-ma-la-DEE
mumps	**les oreillons**	lay-zoh-reh-YOH

pain	**la douleur**	la-doo-LEHR
painful	**douloureux**	doo-loo-REH
painless	**indolore**	eh-doh-LOR
to be ill	**être malade**	aytr ma-LAD

emergency number
le numéro d'urgence
luh-new-may-ROH dewr-ZHAWNS

firefighter
le pompier *m* / la pompière *f*
luh-poh-PYAY / la-poh-PYAYR

policeman
le policier *m* / la policière *f*
luh-poh-lee-SYEH / la-poh-lee-SYEHR

fire engine
le camion de pompier
luh-ka-MYOH duh-poh-PYAY

police car
la voiture de police
la-vwa-TEWR duh-poh-LEES

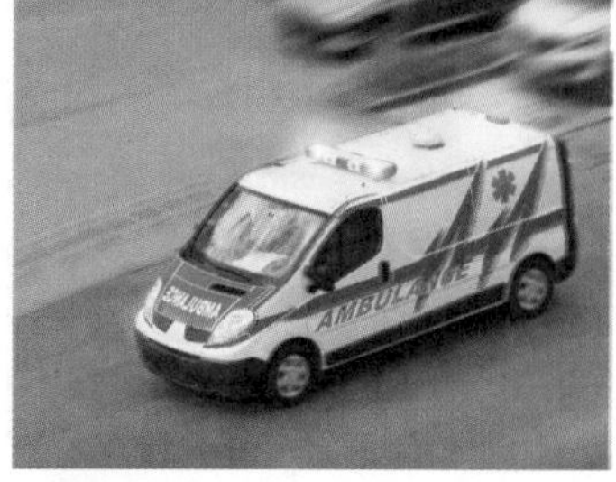

ambulance
l'ambulance
lawn-bew-LOUNS

accident
l'accident
la-xee-DAWN

paramedics
les ambulanciers
lay-zah-bew-loun-SYAY

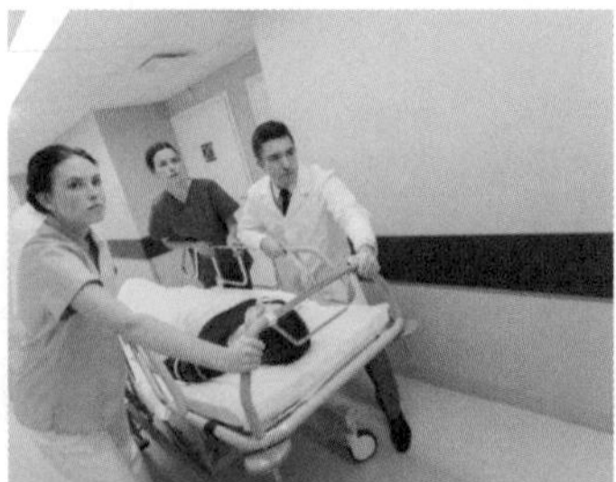

emergency
l'urgence
lewr-ZHAWNS

fire
le feu
luh-feh

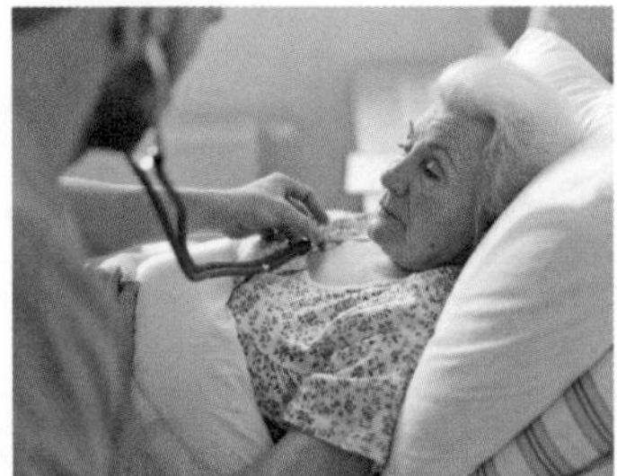

patient
le patient *m* / la patiente *f*
luh-pa-SYEH / la-pa-SYEHT

police
la police
la-poh-LEES

SPORT

badminton racket
la raquette de badminton
la-ra-KAYT duh-bad-meen-TOH

ball
la balle
la-BAL

baseball
la balle de base-ball
la-BAL duh-bayyz-BAL

bicycle
le vélo
luh-vay-LOH

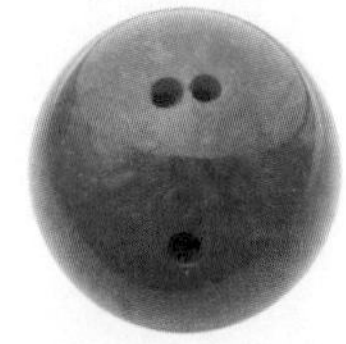

bowling ball
la boule de bowling
la-BOOL duh-bow-LING

cap
la casquette
la-kas-KAYT

football
le ballon de football
luh-ba-LOH duh-foot-BAL

glove
le gant
luh-GOUN

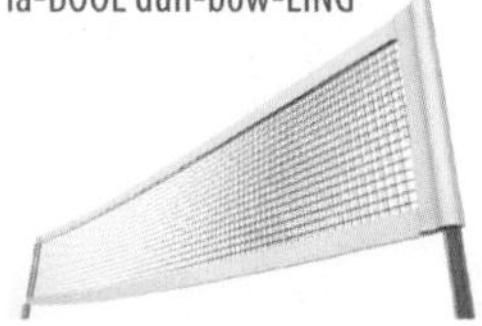

net
le filet
luh-fee-LAY

goggles
les lunettes
lay-lew-NAYT

golf ball
la balle de golf
la-BAL duh-GOLF

helmet
le casque
luh-KASK

goal
le but
luh-BEWT

lane
le couloir
luh-koo-LWAR

hockey puck
le palet de hockey
luh-pa-LAY duh-hoh-KEE

saddle
la selle
la-SAYL

skates
les patins à roulettes
lay-pa-TEH a-roo-LAYT

hockey stick
le bâton de hockey
luh-bah-TOH duh-hoh-KEE

ice-skates
les patins à glace
lya-pa-TEH a-GLAS

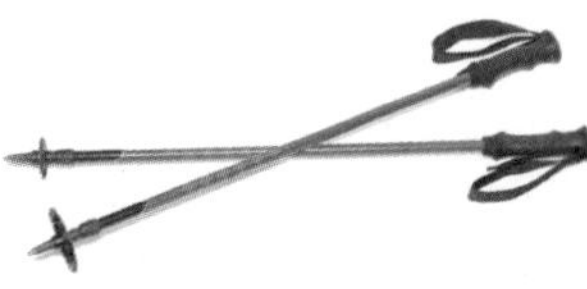

ski poles
les bâtons de ski
lay-bah-TOH duh-SKEE

skis
les skis
lay-SKEE

snowboard
la planche de snowboard
la-PLOUNSH duh-snow-BOARD

surfboard
la planche de surf
la-PLOUNSH duh-SOORF

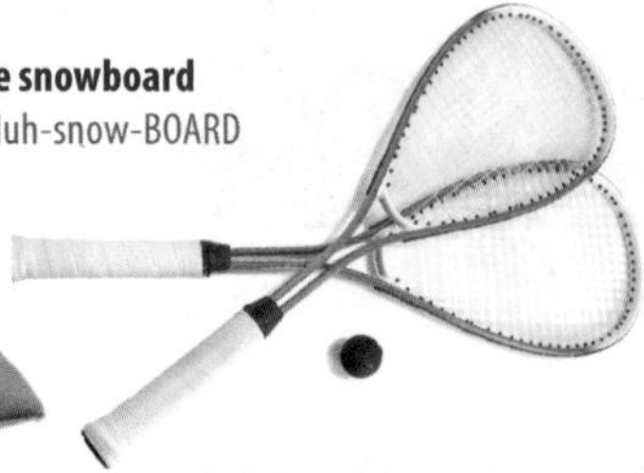

squash racket
la raquette de squash
la-ra-KAYT duh-SKWASH

swimming costume
le maillot de bain
luh-ma-YOH duh-BAH

tennis ball
la balle de tennis
la-BAL duh-teh-NEES

tennis racket
la raquette de tennis
la-ra-KAYT duh-teh-NEES

volleyball
le ballon de volley-ball
luh-ba-LOH duh-voh-ley-BAL

weights
les haltères
lya-zal-TAYR

baseball
le base-ball
luh-baz-BAL

bowling
le bowling
luh-bow-LING

hiking
la randonnée
la-roun-doh-NAY

hockey
le hockey
luh-oh-KEE

cycling
le cyclisme
luh-see-KLEEZM

horseriding
l'équitation
lay-kee-ta-SYOH

football
le football
luh-foot-BAL

running
la course à pied
luh-KOORS a-PYEH

skating
le patinage
luh-pa-tee-NAZH

skiing
le ski
luh-SKEE

swimming
la natation
la-na-ta-SYOH

tennis
le tennis
luh-teh-NEES

volleyball
le volley-ball
luh-voh-layy-BAL

weightlifting
l'haltérophilie
lal-tay-roh-fee-LEE

basketball court
le terrain de basket
luh-teh-REH duh-bas-KAYT

boxing ring
le ring de boxe
luh-RING duh-BOX

fitness centre
le club de sport
luh-KLAB duh-SPOR

football pitch
le terrain de football
luh-teh-REH duh-foot-BAL

golf course
le terrain de golf / le parcours de golf
luh-teh-REH duh-GOLF / luh-par-KOOR duh-GOLF

football ground
le stade de football
luh-STAD duh-foot-BAL

golf club
le club de golf
luh-KLAB duh-GOLF

gym
la salle de sport
la-SAL duh-SPOR

playground
le terrain de jeu
luh-teh-REH duh-ZHEH

racecourse
l'hippodrome
lee-poh-DROM

race track
le circuit de vitesse
luh-seer-KWEE duh-vee-TAYS

recreation area
la zone de loisirs
la-ZON duh-lwa-ZEER

skating rink
la patinoire
la-pa-tee-NWAR

sports ground
le terrain de sport
luh-teh-RAH duh-SPOR

stadium
le stade
luh-STAD

swimming pool
la piscine
la-pee-SEEN

tennis club
le club de tennis
luh-KLAB duh-teh-NEES

tennis court
le court de tennis
luh-KOOR duh-teh-NEES

NATURE

landscape
le paysage
luh-payy-ZAZH

bay
la baie
la-BAY

beach
la plage
la-PLAZH

cave
la grotte
la-GROT

stream
le ruisseau
luh-rew-SOH

desert
le désert
luh-day-ZAYR

earth
la terre
la-TAYR

forest
la forêt
la-foh-REH

woods
le bois
luh-BWA

hill
la colline
la-koh-LEEN

island
l'île
leel

lake
le lac
luh-LAK

mountain
la montagne
la-moh-TANY

ocean
l'océan
loh-say-AH

peak
le sommet
luh-soh-MAY

plain
la plaine
la-PLAYN

pond
l'étang
lay-TOUN

river
la rivière
la-ree-VYAYR

sea
la mer
la-MAYR

brook
le ruisseau
luh-rew-SOH

swamp
le marais
luh-ma-RAY

valley
la vallée
la-va-LAY

waterfall
la chute d'eau
la-SHEWT doh

weather
le temps
luh TAWN

What's the weather like?	**Quel temps fait-il ?**	kayl-TEH fay-TEEL ?
What's the forecast for tomorrow?	**Quelle est la prévision météo pour demain ?**	kayl-AY la-pray-vee-ZYOH may-tay-OH poor duh-MEH ?

blizzard
le blizzard
luh-blee-ZAR

cold
froid
frwa

drizzle
la bruine
la-BREWN

flood
l'inondation
lee-noh-da-SYOH

frost
le givre
luh-ZHEEVR

humidity
l'humidité
lew-mee-dee-TAY

Celsius
Celsius
sehl-SEWS

cyclone
le cyclone
luh-see-KLON

dry
sec
sayk

fog
le brouillard
luh-broo-YAR

hail
la grêle
la-GRAYL

hurricane
l'ouragan
loo-ra-GAH

cloud
le nuage
luh-new-AZH

degree
le degré
luh-duh-GRAY

dry season
la saison sèche
la-say-ZOH saysh

forecast
les prévisions météo
lay-pray-vee-SYOH may-tay-OH

heat
la chaleur
la-sha-LEHR

ice
la glace
la-GLAS

cloudy
nuageux
new-a-ZHEH

dew
la rosée
la-roh-ZAY

Fahrenheit
Fahrenheit
fa-reh-HEIT

freeze
geler
zheh-LAY

hot
chaud
shoh

lightning
la foudre
la-FOODR

rain
la pluie
la-PLWEE

rainy season
la saison des pluies
la-say-SOH day-PLWEE

snowy
neigeux
nay-GEH

temperature
la température
la-teh-pay-ra-TEWR

tsunami
le tsunami
luh-tsoo-na-MEE

rainstorm
l'orage
loh-RAZH

sleet
le grésil
luh-gray-ZEEY

storm
la tempête
la-teh-PAYT

thunder
le tonnerre
luh-toh-nay-REE

typhoon
le typhon
luh-tee-FOH

windy
venteux
vawn-TEH

rainbow
l'arc en ciel
lark-awn-SYAYL

snow
la neige
la-NAYZH

sun
le soleil
luh-soh-LAY

thunderstorm
l'orage
loh-RAZH

warm
chaud
shoh

rainy
pluvieux
plew-VYEH

snowstorm
la tempête de neige
la-teh-PAYT duh-NAYZH

sunny
ensoleillé
awn-soh-lay-YAY

tornado
la tornade
la-tor-NAD

wind
le vent
luh-VAWN

pet owner
le propriétaire de l'animal
luh-pro-pryeh-TAYR deh la-nee-MAL

aquarium
l'aquarium
la-kwa-REWM

cage
la cage
la-KAZH

canary
le canari
luh-ka-na-REE

bird
l'oiseau
lwa-ZOH

dog
le chien
luh-SHYEH

pet shop
l'animalerie
la-nee-ma-lay-REE

fish
le poisson
luh-pwa-SOH

cat
le chat
luh-SHA

gecko
le gecko
luh-geh-KOH

hamster
le hamster
luh-am-STAYR

guinea pig
le cochon d'Inde
luh-koh-SHOH dehd

lizard
le lézard
luh-lay-ZAR

rabbit
le lapin
luh-la-PEH

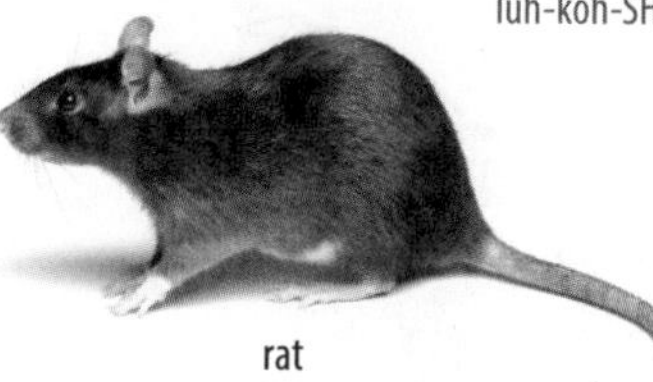

rat
le rat
luh-RA

mouse
la souris
la-soo-REE

parrot
le perroquet
luh-peh-roh-KAY

snake
le serpent
luh-sayr-POUN

spider
l'araignée
la-ray-NYAY

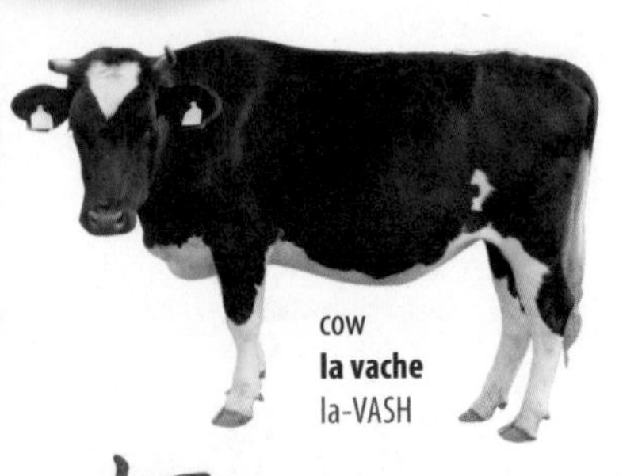

cow
la vache
la-VASH

chicken
le poulet
luh-poo-LAY

donkey
l'âne
lan

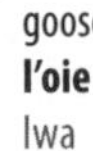

goose
l'oie
lwa

goat
la chèvre
la-SHAYVR

horse
le cheval
luh-shay-VAL

sheep
le mouton
luh-moo-TOH

duck
le canard
luh-kah-NAR

rabbit
le lapin
luh-la-PEH

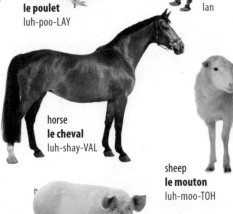

pig
le cochon
luh-koh-SHOH

turkey
la dinde
la-dehnd

giraffe
la girafe
la-zhee-RAF
elephant
l'éléphant
lay-lay-FOUN
jaguar
le jaguar
luh-zha-goo-AR
tiger
le tigre
luh-TEEGR
lion
le lion
luh-LYOH
leopard
le léopard
luh-lay-oh-PAR
puma
le puma
luh-pew-MA

hippopotamus
l'hippopotame
lee-poh-poh-TAM

monkey
le singe
luh-SEHZH

chimpanzee
le chimpanzé
luh-sheh-poun-ZAY

ostrich
l'autruche
loh-TREWSH

rhinoceros
le rhinocéros
luh-ree-noh-say-ROS

armadillo
le tatou
luh-ta-TOO

sloth
le paresseux
luh-pa-ra-SEH

iguana
l'iguane
lee-GWAN

kangaroo
le kangourou
luh-koun-goo-ROO

bear
l'ours
loors

zebra
le zèbre
luh-ZAYBR

hyena
la hyène
la-YAYN

seal
le phoque
luh-FOK

gazelle
la gazelle
la-ga-ZAYL

antelope
l'antilope
loun-tee-LOP

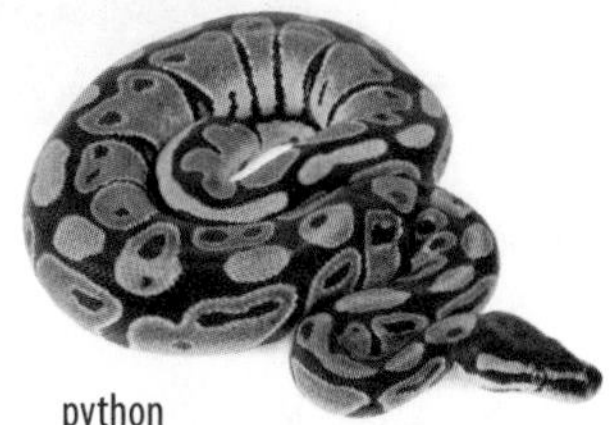

python
le python
luh-pee-TOH

water buffalo
le buffle
luh-BEWFL

boar
le sanglier
luh-soun-glee-YAY

cobra
le cobra
luh-koh-BRA

whale
la baleine
la-ba-LAYN

killer whale
l'orque
lork

shark
le requin
luh-roh-KEH

turtle
la tortue
la-tor-TEW

dolphin
le dauphin
luh-doh-FEH

crocodile
le crocodile
luh-kroh-koh-DEEL

SHOPPING AND SERVICES

grocery store
l'épicerie
lay-pee-seh-REE

bazaar
le bazar
luh-ba-ZAR

bookshop
la librairie
la-leeb-ray-REE

computer shop
le magasin d'électronique
luh-ma-ga-ZEH day-layk-troh-NEEK

corner shop
l'épicerie du coin
lay-pee-seh-REE dew-KZEH

farmers' market
le marché de producteurs
luh-mar-SHAY duh-proh-dewk-TEHR

flea market
le marché aux puces
luh-mar-SHAY oh-PEWS

flower market
le marché aux fleurs
luh-mar-SHAY oh-FLEHR

bakery
la boulangerie
la-boo-loun-zjay-REE

fruit stall
le stand de fruits
luh-STOUND duh-FRWEE

market
le marché
luh-mar-SHAY

newsagent
le marchand de journaux
luh-mar-SHOUN duh-zhoor-NOH

shoe shop
le magasin de chaussures
luh-ma-ga-ZEH duh-shoh-SEWR

street vendor
le vendeur de rue
luh-vawn-DEHR duh-REW

supermarket
le supermarché
luh-sew-payr-mar-SHAY

department store	**le grand magasin**	luh-GROUN ma-ga-ZEH
shopping centre	**le centre commercial**	luh-SAWNTR koh-mayr-SYAL

sale
les soldes
lay-SOLD

checkout / till checkout
la caisse
la-KAYS

conveyor belt
le tapis roulant
luh-ta-PEE roo-LOUN

customer
le client *m* / la cliente *f*
luh-klee-EH / la-klee-EHT

price
le prix
luh-PREE

queue
la file d'attente
la-FEEL da-AWNT

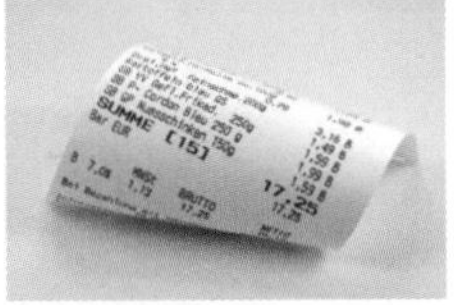

receipt
le reçu
luh-reh-SEW

cashier
le caissier *m* / la caissière *f*
luh-kay-SYAY / la-ka-SYAYR

shopping bag
le sac
luh-SAK

shopping list
la liste des courses
la-LEEST day-KOORS

shopping basket
le panier
luh-pa-NYAY

trolley
le chariot
luh-sha-RYOH

bill for	**la facture pour**	la-fak-TEWR poor
goods	**les achats**	lay-za-SHA
shopper	**l'acheteur *m* / l'acheteuse *f***	lash-TUHR / lash-TUHZ
to cost	**coûter**	koo-TAY
to get a great bargain	**faire une bonne affaire**	fayr ewn bon-a-FAYR
to purchase	**acheter**	ash-TAY
to queue	**faire la queue**	fayr la-KUH
Can I help you?	**Puis-je vous aider ?**	pweezh-VOO zay-DAY ?

belt
la ceinture
la-seh-TEWR

boots
les bottes
lay-BOT

coat
le manteau
luh-moun-TOH

raincoat
l'imperméable
leh-payr-may-ABL

hat
le chapeau
luh-sha-POH

gloves
les gants
lay-GOUN

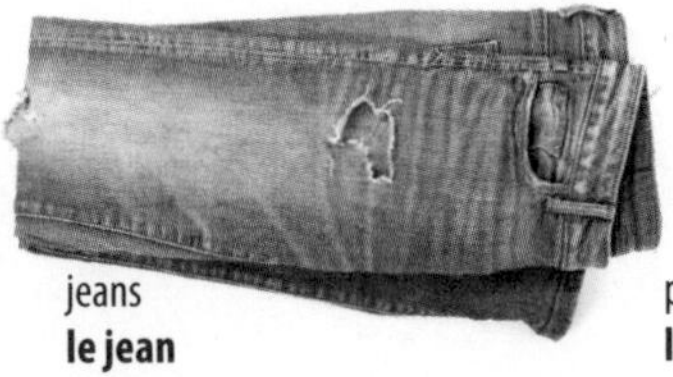

jeans
le jean
luh-JEEN

pyjamas
le pyjama
luh-pee-zha-MA

jacket
le blouson
luh-blooZOHT

shoes
les chaussures
lay-shoh-SEWR

jumper
le pull
luh-PEWL

scarf
l'écharpe
lay-SHARP

underwear
les sous-vêtements
lay-soo-vay-tay-MAWN

tie
la cravate
la-kra-VAT

sweatshirt
le sweatshirt
luh-sweet-SHAYRT

briefs
le slip
luh-SLEEP

shirt
la chemise
la-sheh-MEEZ

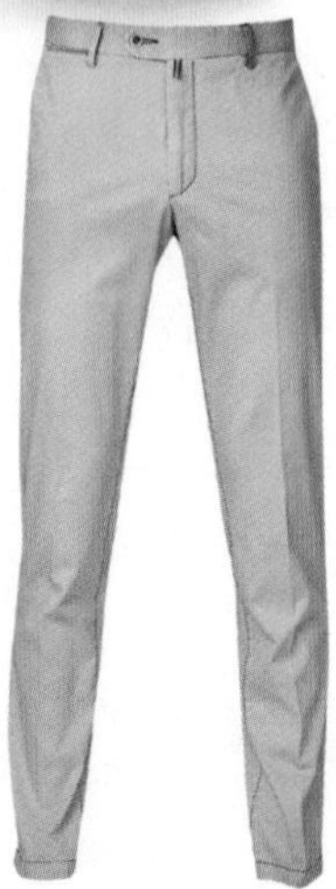

trousers
le pantalon
luh-poun-ta-LOH

t-shirt
le T-shirt
luh-tee-SHAYRT

socks
les chaussettes
lay-shoh-SAYT

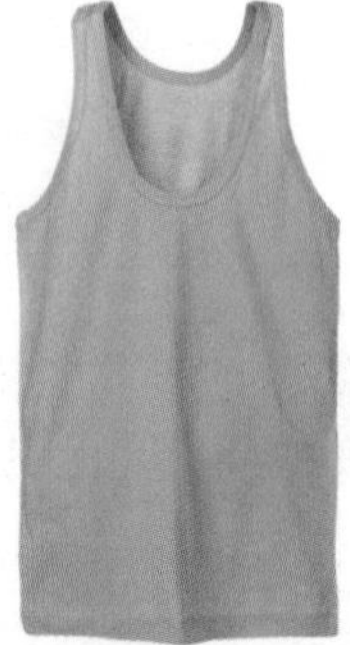

undershirt
le maillot de corps
luh-ma-YOH duh-KOR

slippers
les chaussons
lya-shoh-SOH

suit
le costume
luh-kos-TEWM

He has a hat on.	**Il porte un chapeau.**	eel-PORT eh-sha-POH.
These briefs are the right size.	**Ce slip est de la bonne taille.**	seh-SLEEP ay duh-la-BON tay
What did he have on?	**Qu'est-ce qu'il portait ?**	kays-KEEL por-TAY ?
I want these boxer shorts in a size 42.	**Je veux ce caleçon en taille 42.**	zhuh veh ceh ka-lay-SOH uh-TAY ka-rount-DEH

jacket
le blouson
luh-blooZOHT

boots
les bottes
lay-BOT

gloves
les gants
lay-GOUN

hat
le chapeau
luh-sha-POH

raincoat
l'imperméable
leh-pehr-may-ABL

coat
le manteau
luh-moun-TOH

jeans
le jean
luh-JEEN

pyjamas
le pyjama
luh-pee-zha-MA

belt
la ceinture
la-seh-TEWR

dress
la robe
la-ROB

scarf
le foulard
luh-foo-LAR

jumper
le pull
luh-PEWL

pants
la culotte
la-kew-LOT

skirt
la jupe
la-ZHEWP

shoes
les chaussures
lay-shoh-SEWR

sweatshirt
le sweatshirt
luh-sweet-SHAYRT

socks
les chaussettes
lay-shoh-SAYT

shirt
la chemise
la-shay-MEEZ

stockings
les bas
lay-BA

t-shirt
le T-shirt
luh tee-SHAYRT

trousers
le pantalon
luh-poun-ta-LOH

slacks
le pantalon
luh-poun-ta-LOH

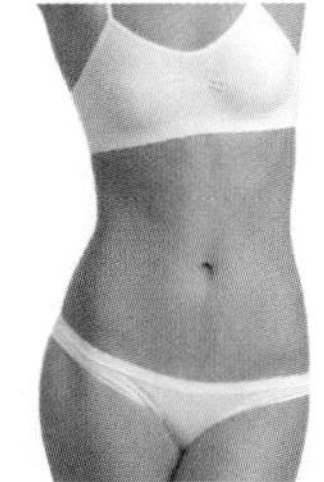

underwear
les sous-vêtements
lay-soo-vay-tay-MAWN

bra
le soutien-gorge
luh-soo-tyeh-GORZH

slippers
les chaussons
lay-shoh-SOH

She has a hat on.	**Elle porte un chapeau.**	ayl port eh-sha-POH
The dress looks nice on you.	**La robe vous va bien.**	la-ROB voo-va-BYEH.
What did she have on?	**Qu'est-ce qu'elle portait ?**	kays-KAYL por-TAY ?
I want these boots in a size 38.	**Je veux ces bottes en taille 38.**	zheh-VEH lay-BOT awn-TAY trawnt-WEET

suit
le costume
luh-kos-TEWM

car repair shop
le garage
luh-ga-RAZH

barber shop
le barbier
leh-bar-BYAY

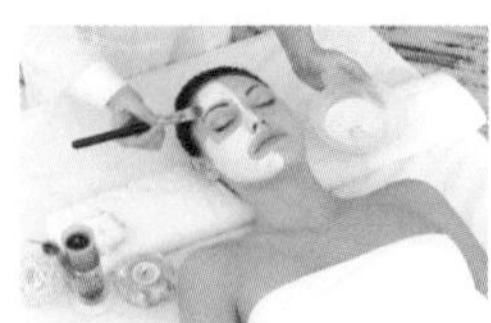

beauty salon
le salon de beauté
luh-sa-LOH duh-boh-TAY

bicycle repair shop
l'atelier de réparation de vélos
la-teh-LYAY deh ray-pa-ra-SYOH duh-vay-LOH

watchmaker
l'horloger *m* / l'horlogère *f*
lor-lo-ZHAY / lor-lo-ZHAYR

laundromat
la laverie automatique
la-la-vay-REE oh-toh-ma-TEEK

dry cleaners
le pressing
luh-pray-SEENG

locksmiths
la serrurerie
la-eh-rew-ray-REE

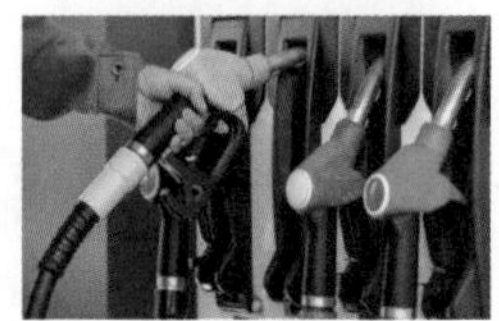

petrol station
la station essence
la-sta-SYOH ay-SAWNS

12

CULTURE AND MEDIA

blog
le blog
luh-BLOG

to broadcast
transmettre
troun-SMAYTR

magazine
le magazine
luh-ma-ga-ZEEN

newspaper
le journal
luh-zhoor-NAL

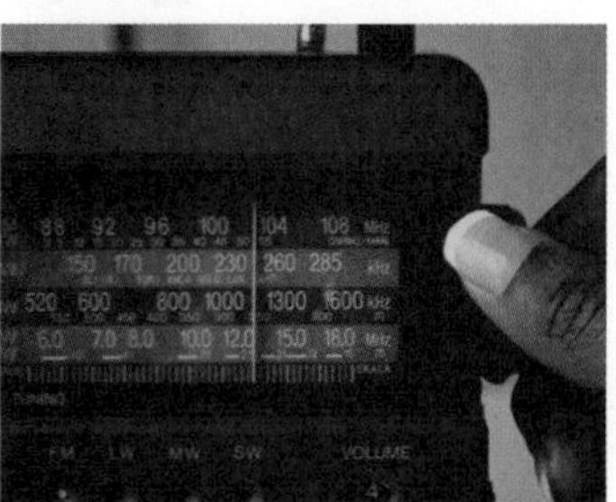

radio
la radio
la-ra-DYOH

television
la télévision
la-tay-lay-vee-ZYOH

news broadcast
le journal télévisé
luh-zjoor-NAL tay-lay-vee-ZAY

weather forecast
la météo
la-may-tay-OH

blogosphere	**la blogosphère**	la-bloh-goh-SFAYR
mass media	**les médias**	lay-may-DYA
news	**les nouvelles**	lay-noo-VAYL
press	**la presse**	la-PRAYS
tabloid	**la presse à scandale**	la-PRAYS a skouh-DAL
programme	**le programme / l 'émission**	luh-proh-GRAM / lay-mee-SYOH
soap	**le feuilleton**	luh-feh-yeh-TOH
drama	**le drame**	luh-DRAM
series	**la série**	la-say-REE
film	**le film**	luh-FEELM
documentary	**le documentaire**	luh-dohkew-mawn-TAYR
music programme	**le programme musical**	luh-proh-GRAM mew-zee-KAL
sports programme	**le programme sportif**	luh-proh-GRAM spor-TEEF
talk show	**l'émission-débat**	lay-mee-SYOH day-BA
episode	**l'épisode**	lay-pee-SOHD
business news	**l'actualité économique**	lak-tew-a-lee-TAY ay-koh-noh-MEEK
sports report	**le reportage sportif**	luh-reh-por-TAZH spor-TEEF
book review	**la critique littéraire**	la-kree-TEEK lee-tay-RAYR
ad / advertisement	**la publicité**	la-pew-blee-see-TAY

message
le message
luh-may-SAZH

address / URL
l'adresse / l'URL
la-DRAYS / LEW-AYR-AYL

application / app
l'application / l'appli
la-plee-ka-SYOH / la-PLEE

network
le réseau
luh-reh-SOH

inbox	**la boîte de réception**	la-BWAT deh ray-sayp-SYOH
IP address	**l'adresse IP**	la-DRAYS EE-PEH
internet	**l'internet**	eh-tayr-NAYT
website	**le site internet**	luh-SEET eh-tayr-NAYT
mail	**le mail**	luh-MAYYL
search engine	**le moteur de recherche**	luh-moh-TEHR deh reh-SHAYRSH
to search	**rechercher**	reh-shayr-SHAY
to share	**partager**	par-ta-ZHAY
to log in	**se connecter**	seh ko-nayk-TAY

to send
envoyer
awn-vwa-YAY

login
le nom d'utilisateur
luh-NOH dew-tee-lee-za-TEHR

to log out
se déconnecter
seh day-koh-nayk-TAY

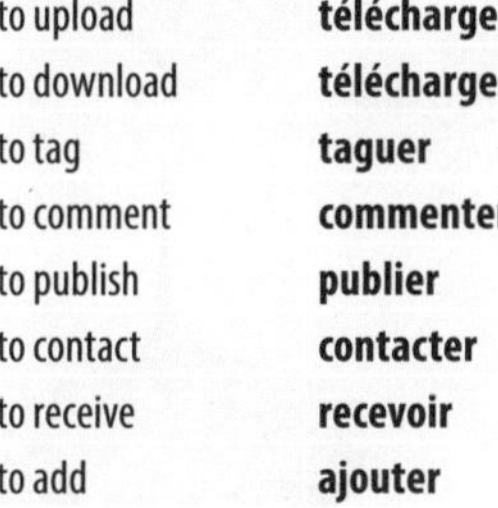

to upload	**télécharger vers**	tay-lay-shar-ZHAY vayr
to download	**télécharger de**	tay-lay-shar-ZHAY
to tag	**taguer**	ta-GAY
to comment	**commenter**	kom-mawn-TAY
to publish	**publier**	pew-blee-YAY
to contact	**contacter**	koh-tak-TAY
to receive	**recevoir**	reh-seh-VWAR
to add	**ajouter**	a-zhoo-TAY

link
le lien
luh-LYEH

CD
le CD
luh CAY-DAY

CD-ROM
le CD-ROM
luh SAY-DAY-ROM

DVD
le DVD
luh DAY-VAY-DAY

mouse
la souris
la-soo-REE

keyboard
le clavier
luh-kla-VYEH

USB flash drive
la clé USB
la-KLAY EW-AYS-BAY

laptop
le portable
luh-por-TABL

modem
le modem
luh-moh-DAYM

monitor
le moniteur
luh-moh-nee-TEHR

router
le routeur
luh-roo-TEHR

tablet
la tablette
la-ta-BLAYT

printer
l'imprimante
leh-pree-MOUT

scanner
le scanner
luh-ska-NAYR

to copy	**copier**	koh-PYAY
to delete	**effacer**	ay-fa-SAY
desktop	**le bureau**	luh-bew-ROH
file	**le fichier**	luh-fee-SHYAY
folder	**le dossier**	luh-doh-SYEH
offline	**hors ligne**	ohr-LEENY
online	**en ligne**	uh-LEENY
password	**le mot de passe**	luh-MO d-PAS

to print	**imprimer**	eh-pree-MAY
to save	**sauvegarder**	sohv-gar-DAY
to scan	**scanner**	ska-NAY
screenshot	**la capture d'écran**	la-kap-TEWR day-KROUW
server	**le serveur**	luh-sehr-VEHR
software	**le logiciel**	luh-loh-zhee-SYAYL
to undo	**annuler**	a-new-LAY
virus	**le virus**	luh-vee-REWS

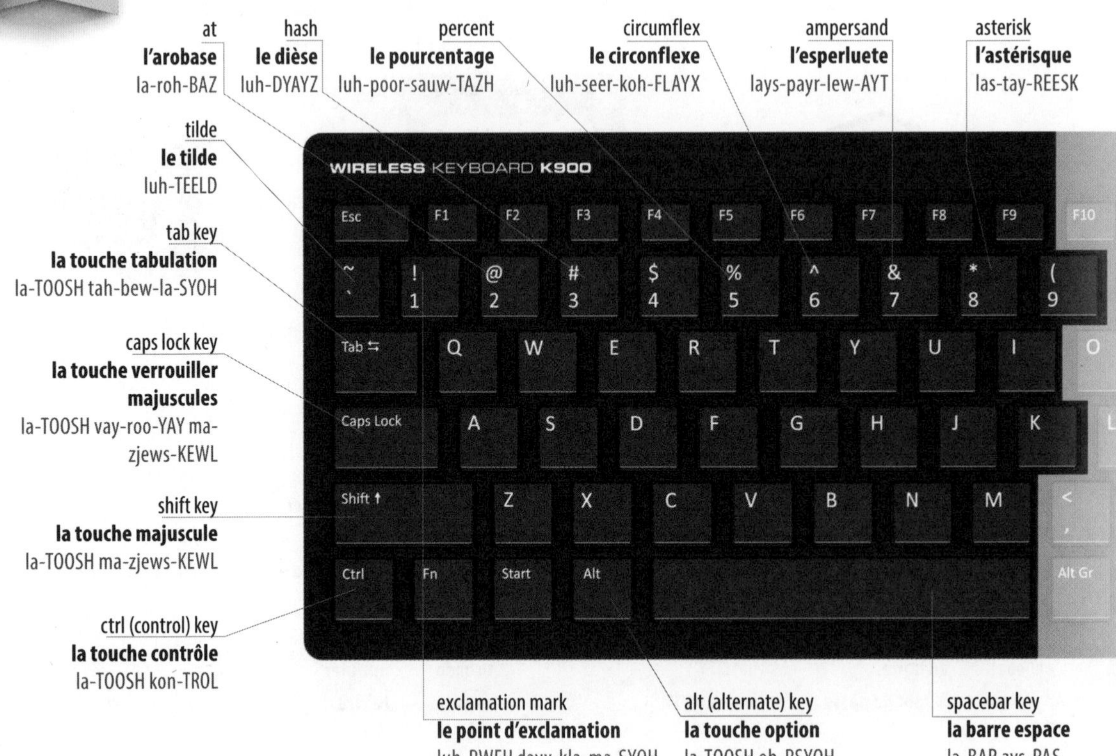
at
l'arobase
la-roh-BAZ
hash
le dièse
luh-DYAYZ
percent
le pourcentage
luh-poor-sauw-TAZH
circumflex
le circonflexe
luh-seer-koh-FLAYX
ampersand
l'esperluete
lays-payr-lew-AYT
asterisk
l'astérisque
las-tay-REESK
tilde
le tilde
luh-TEELD
tab key
la touche tabulation
la-TOOSH tah-bew-la-SYOH
caps lock key
la touche verrouiller majuscules
la-TOOSH vay-roo-YAY ma-zjews-KEWL
shift key
la touche majuscule
la-TOOSH ma-zjews-KEWL
ctrl (control) key
la touche contrôle
la-TOOSH kon-TROL
exclamation mark
le point d'exclamation
luh-PWEH dayx-kla-ma-SYOH
alt (alternate) key
la touche option
la-TOOSH oh-PSYOH
spacebar key
la barre espace
la-BAR ays-PAS
WIRELESS KEYBOARD K900
Esc
F1
F2
F3
F4
F5
F6
F7
F8
F9
F10
~ `
! 1
@ 2
# 3
$ 4
% 5
^ 6
& 7
* 8
(9
Tab
Q
W
E
R
T
Y
U
I
O
Caps Lock
A
S
D
F
G
H
J
K
L
Shift
Z
X
C
V
B
N
M
Ctrl
Fn
Start
Alt
Alt Gr

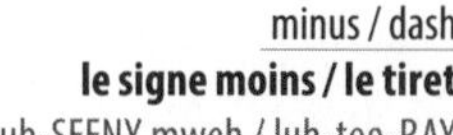

minus / dash
le signe moins / le tiret
luh-SEENY mweh / luh-tee-RAY

plus
le signe plus
luh-SEENY plews

equal
le signe égal
luh-SEENY ay-GAL

colon
les deux points
lay deh pweh

semicolon
le point-virgule
luh-PWEH veer-GEWL

dot / full stop
le point
luh-PWEH

question mark
le point d'interrogation
luh-PWEH deh-tay-roh-gah-SYOH

enter key
la touche entrée
la-TOOSH awn-TRAY

forward slash
la barre oblique
la-BAR oh-BLEEK

back slash
la barre oblique inversée
la-BAR oh-BLEEK eh-vayr-SAY

backspace key
la touche retour arrière
la-TOOSH reh-TOOR a-RYAYR

delete or del key
la touche supprimer
la-TOOSH sew-pree-MAY

amusement park
le parc d'attractions
luh-PARK da-tra-XYOH

aquarium
l'aquarium
la-kwa-REWM

art gallery
la galerie d'art
la-ga-lay-REE dar

art museum
le musée d'art
luh-mew-ZAY dar

botanical garden
le jardin botanique
luh-zhar-DEH boh-ta-NEEK

cinema
le cinéma
luh-see-nay-MA

circus
le cirque
luh-SEERK

discotheque
la discothèque
la-dees-koh-TAYK

garden
le jardin
luh-zhar-DEH

night club
la boîte de nuit
la-BWAT duh-NWEE

trade fair / trade show
la foire commerciale / le salon professionel
la-FWAR-kom-mayr-SYAL / luh-sa-LOH pro-fay-syo-NAYL

opera house
l'opéra
luh-pay-RA

concert hall
la salle de concert
la-SAL duh kon-SAYR

park
le parc
luh-PARK

planetarium
le planétarium
luh-pla-nay-ta-REWM

science museum
le musée des sciences
luh-mew-ZAY day-SYAWNS

sights
les sites d'intérêt
lay-SEET deh-tay-RAY

theatre
le théâtre
luh-tay-ATR

tourist attraction
l'attraction touristique
la-trak-SYON too-rees-TEEK

water park
le parc aquatique
luh-PARK a-kwa-TEEK

zoo
le zoo
luh-ZOO

accordion
l'accordéon
la-kor-day-OH

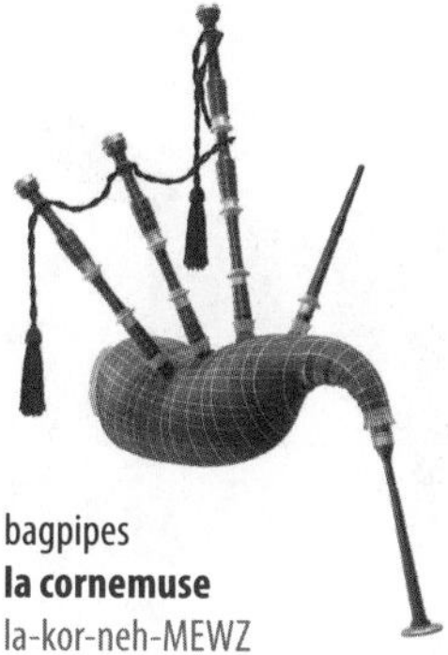

bagpipes
la cornemuse
la-kor-neh-MEWZ

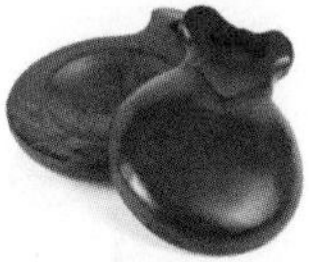

castanets
les castagnettes
lay-kas-ta-NYAYT

cello
le violoncelle
luh-vioh-loh-TCHAYL

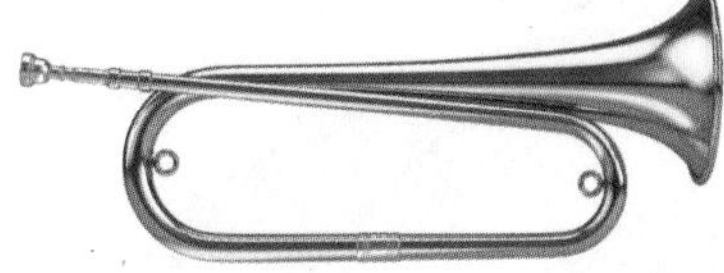

bugle
le clairon
luh-klay-ROH

banjo
le banjo
luh-ban-ZHOH

clarinet
la clarinette
la-kla-ree-NAYT

cymbal
la cymbale
la-seh-BAL

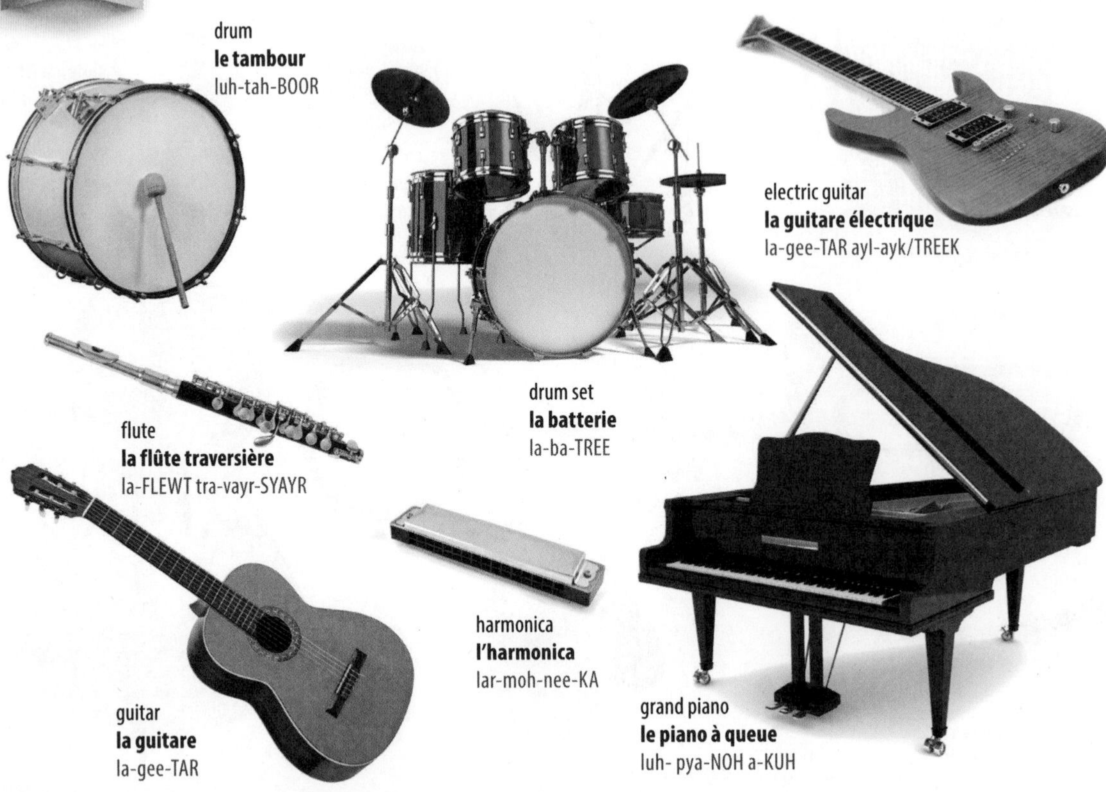

drum
le tambour
luh-tah-BOOR

electric guitar
la guitare électrique
la-gee-TAR ayl-ayk/TREEK

drum set
la batterie
la-ba-TREE

flute
la flûte traversière
la-FLEWT tra-vayr-SYAYR

harmonica
l'harmonica
lar-moh-nee-KA

guitar
la guitare
la-gee-TAR

grand piano
le piano à queue
luh- pya-NOH a-KUH

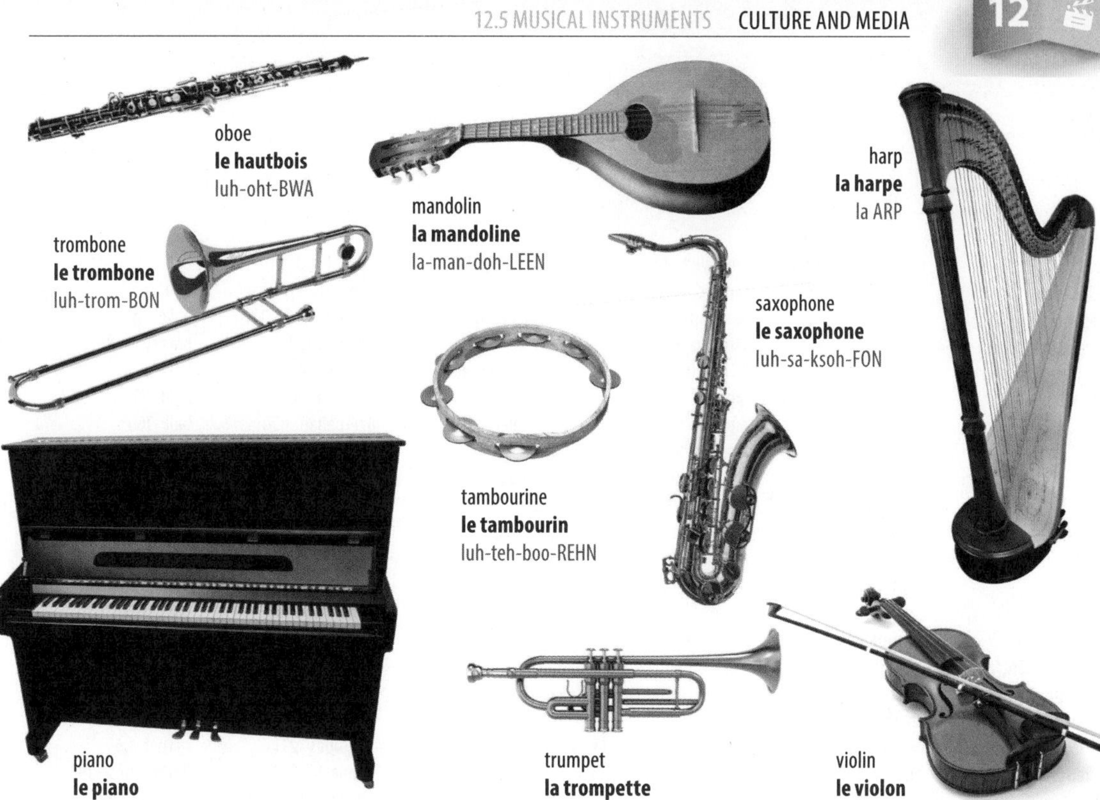

oboe
le hautbois
luh-oht-BWA

mandolin
la mandoline
la-man-doh-LEEN

harp
la harpe
la ARP

trombone
le trombone
luh-trom-BON

saxophone
le saxophone
luh-sa-ksoh-FON

tambourine
le tambourin
luh-teh-boo-REHN

piano
le piano
luh-pya-NOH

trumpet
la trompette
la-trom-PAYT

violin
le violon
luh vyoh-LOH

Index

C

G

H

U

V